CARING
FOR LIFE
AND DEATH

CARING
FOR LIFE
AND DEATH

Nelda Samarel
Associate Professor
Department of Nursing
William Paterson College
Wayne, NJ 07470

TAYLOR & FRANCIS

CARING FOR LIFE AND DEATH

The quotation on p. 135 is reproduced with permission from Benoliel, J. Q. (1972). The Concept of Care for a Child with Leukemia. *Nursing Forum,* 11(2):194–204.

2 3 4 5 6 7 8 9 0   B R B R   9 8 7 6 5 4 3

This book was set in Times Roman by Hemisphere Publishing Corporation. The editors were Steve Kennedy and Joyce Duncan; the production supervisor was Peggy M. Rote; and the typesetters were Phoebe A. Carter and Deborah J. Hamblen. Cover design by Debra Eubanks Riffe.
Printing and binding by Braun-Brumfield, Inc.

A CIP catalog record for this book is available from the British Library.

Library of Congress Cataloging-in-Publication Data

Samarel, Nelda
    Caring for life and death / Nelda Samarel.
        p.   cm.—(Series in death education, aging, and health care)
    Includes bibliographical references and index.

    1. Terminal care.   I. Series.
    [DNLM: 1. Critical Care—methods.   2. Nursing Caring—methods.
    3. Terminal Care—methods.   WY 86 S187c]
    RT87.T45S26   1991
    362.1'75—dc20   90-15659
                                                                       CIP

    ISBN 1-56032-124-5
    ISSN 0275-3510

For Jack,
The Wind Beneath My Wings

Contents

Preface

In any setting, on any shift, a nurse cares for several types of patients: She must fight death for acutely ill patients while caring for the dying; she must assist patients experiencing acute psychiatric episodes while helping patients who are chronically impaired; she must care for mothers of healthy newborns while comforting mothers of aborted fetuses. These are but a few examples of the dichotomies of care faced by the nurse. Each day she cares for mutually exclusive groups of patients with diverse needs. How does she manage to meet the disparate needs of the patients in her charge?

In this study, I explore how nurses care for and attempt to meet the needs of two mutually exclusive groups of patients: terminally ill patients in the last stages of illness and acutely ill patients expected to recover. The exploration gives rise to two pivotal questions: Are there differences in the ways nurses care for the living and the dying? Do the disparate needs of the two groups result in role conflict for the nurses who care for them?

I found that the two factors influencing the ways nurses care for their patients are (1) the patient's level of consciousness (that is, whether or not the patient is responsive), and (2) the "busyness," or amount of work required by each nurse on any given day. This study also reveals that nurses who develop a philosophy of death, participate in regular support groups and continuing education programs, and have time to enact and reflect upon their caring behaviors are best able to make the transition between different types of patients and to give the care that is required of them. In this book I explore how these nurses make their transitions and discuss the implications of these findings for effective nursing education and patient care.

Chapter 1 explores the concept of nurses as actors playing a variety of roles. A significant difference between actors and nurses, however, is that actors play one role at a time, whereas nurses play several simultaneously. Is it possible to be cast simultaneously in multiple roles without risking role conflict? An ethnographic method is used to explore this problem within the theoretical perspective of symbolic interactionism, the focus of which is the social and psychological aspects of reality. In an interactionist perspective, a nurse's actions are behavioral and verbal responses to the symbolic acts of her patients.

In the second chapter the reader is introduced to the setting in which nurses care for the living and the dying. I describe a hospital unit known as Four South, its patients, and its nurses, with whom the reader will become quite familiar in the next chapter.

Five days in the world of Four South are presented in Chapter 3 in the form of a script that reveals the ways in which the nurses manage their work routine, relate to each other, handle the stresses of their personal and professional lives, and deal with the issues of life and death confronted by their patients. It becomes apparent that the Four South nurses deal day to day with the most fundamental and poignant issues facing humanity: living and dying.

The ways in which these nurses care for their patients reflect the ways in which they live their lives, that is, their philosophies of life, living, and death. Each nurse on Four South has given considerable thought to the issues of life and death and applies this philosophy to her nursing care. In Chapter 4 I focus on the nurses' personal values and their beliefs about nursing. I examine the relationship between their expressed beliefs and values and their nursing care.

Chapter 5 explores the ways nurses meet the differing needs of their patients. When nurses care for two mutually exclusive groups of patients, as the Four South nurses do, a natural question arises about the differences and similarities in the patients' needs. Four South nurses believe that unresponsive patients have different needs than responsive patients, regardless of whether they are "acute" or "terminal." Nursing behaviors vary with patients' levels of responsiveness. For example, in interactions with unresponsive patients, nursing behaviors are predominantly nonverbal.

In Chapter 6 I focus on the way nurses care for their patients, both the dying and the acutely ill. Although a brief discussion of role theory might lead us to conclude that these nurses would experience role conflict in caring for the two groups of patients, an analysis of their care reveals a smooth role transition without the expected role conflict. I suggest that the commonality of caring explains the absence of conflict in caring for acutely and terminally ill patients. Humanistic caring, or caring *about* the patients, forms the core of all nursing philosophies. While a complete absence of caring is never observed in any interaction, the extent of the caring within interactions does vary with the degree of "busyness," or amount of work required, of the nurse at any particular time; the busier the nurse, the less time available for caring behaviors. Busyness, as a dynamic, has a direct impact on the ways nurses interact with their patients, whether acutely or terminally ill. The busier the nurse, the less time available to enact and reflect upon her caring behaviors.

In Chapter 7 I discuss this study's contribution to our understanding of the ways nurses simultaneously meet the needs of different types of patients. The findings of the study have implications for the increasing numbers of patients who survive head injuries, strokes, and other neurological insults. Many of these patients experience transient or permanent alterations in their levels of consciousness. The understanding gained from an exploration of nurses' caring behaviors for responsive and unresponsive patients may dramatically affect nursing care for these patients. Notably, the findings of this study differ from those suggested in the literature. The most common view found in the literature is that nurses caring for the terminally ill attempt to protect themselves by developing a callous exterior and assuming attitudes of exaggerated detachment. I found that the Four South nurses did not appear detached or to avoid dying situations. I discuss the reasons for these differences and the implications for future research in this important area.

Appendix A is a description of the research design and method used in the study. Appendix B is a personal account of my experience in the research process, beginning with a brief glimpse into my background and continuing through the fieldwork process. I discuss the methodological problems confronted during the study as well as what I learned through this experience. Appendix C is a review of the past literature relevant to the study, specifically literature related to hospices and to caring.

Nelda Samarel

Acknowledgments

This book is based on my doctoral dissertation research. I offer my sincere appreciation to David Carr, Ph.D., who, as chairperson of my dissertation committee, offered his continuous support, guidance, and encouragement.

I am grateful to my husband, Jack, and children, Michael, Donna, and Adam, for their patience, support, and understanding on all the evenings that they arrived home to the sound of the word-processor rather than to the aroma of dinner.

I owe a debt to the patients and staff of the hospice where the data were collected. Without their cooperation, this study would not have been completed.

During the period of observation I was struck by the qualitative aspects of both the hospice personnel and the hospice climate. The nurses demonstrated a deep personal commitment to helping that was manifested in their involvement and in their sharing of self with patients. I saw demonstrations of professional competence, sensitivity, and compassion for their patients, even when confronted with crises in their own lives. I saw examples of caring that captured the qualities of nursing I most admire.

In the process of observing a group of nurses care for the living and the dying, I learned much about life. For this, I thank them.

Nelda Samarel

Chapter 1

Introduction

NURSES AS ACTORS

The call bell rings for Room 406. The nurse, sipping a cup of coffee that is a substitute for a delayed lunch, interrupts her short-lived break and attends to the patient. Terminally ill Mrs. Olive is again experiencing pain in her abdomen. When the nurse enters Mrs. Olive's room, she sees a frail, middle-aged woman clutching the bedcovers as she lies immobile waiting for some assurance that something can be done to relieve what seems like unrelenting suffering. One glance at the nurse's face and Mrs. Olive knows that her pain is understood. She knows, too, that this nurse understands the fear she is experiencing, fear of her uncertain future. The nurse assures Mrs. Olive that medication to relieve the pain will be provided immediately.

On her way from Mrs. Olive's room to obtain the medication, the nurse is called into another room. Elderly Mr. Hays is sitting up in bed. He has an anxious expression on his face and grabs the nurse's hand as she approaches his bed. In agitated tones he asks,

When are they (my family) coming? They haven't been here and its getting late. I'm all alone and no one is coming. They don't know I'm here (in the hospital) or they'd be here with me. Please call them.

The nurse gently explains to a confused Mr. Hays that it is only 1:00 p.m., and his family visits daily at dinner time. She reminds him that they visited the previous day and promised to return today. As she holds his hand in hers, she explains that they will be visiting in a few hours and that he is not alone. Mr. Hays's body and facial expression relax noticeably as he is again reminded that he is not "alone." The nurse quickly continues to the medication room to obtain Mrs. Olive's medication.

A few moments later, the nurse returns to Mrs. Olive with the pain medication. After the injection, the nurse assists Mrs. Olive to a comfortable position and places a cool washcloth on her forehead. She remains at the bedside, firmly holding Mrs. Olive's hand in her own. She withdraws her hand only to change the cool washcloth. Fifteen minutes later, when Mrs. Olive is asleep, the nurse quietly leaves the room. On her way back to the nurses' station she checks on Mr. Hays. He, too, is comfortable.

As the nurse passes Ms. Cordrey's room, she hears her name called. She enters the room to find a jubilant young woman who immediately exclaims,

Guess what? The tests have all come back and I'm clean! No cancer anywhere! I was so worried before and now I feel like I'm on top of the world!

With this, the young woman throws her arms around the nurse. The nurse responds with a bear hug and they both laugh as they chatter about the fact that both "really knew" that Ms. Cordrey's tests would be fine.

When the nurse returns to Mrs. Olive's room the next morning, Mrs. Olive thanks her for her help the previous day,

I don't know what I'd do without you girls (nurses). You *really* understand and are always so supportive. It's not just giving the injections; it's the way you care. I can see it on your face and it makes me feel like I can get through it (the pain).

Who is this nurse? To her patients, she appears to be compassionate, understanding, pleasant, gentle, and always there to meet their needs. But who *is* she? What her patients do not know is that she was present when the young mother in the next room was told she had inoperable brain cancer. Or that she has just been with the family of a young man who died earlier in the day. Or that her husband told her the previous evening that he was leaving her. Or that her son has just become engaged to be married. Or that she has become a grandmother for the first time. This nurse is a human being who experiences life's normal trials and tribulations, as well as its joys and celebrations.

The nurse must leave behind her personal problems, as well as her personal joys, when she enters her patient's room. To meet her patient's needs and convey compassion and understanding, her own needs must be temporarily set aside. She must also set aside her thoughts and feelings about other patients. When Mrs. Olive is in pain and fearful that the pain will be unrelieved, the last thing she wishes to see is a cheerful nurse celebrating the birth of a grandchild. Nor does she wish to see a nurse teary and depressed about her own marital problems. And, certainly, Ms. Cordrey does not wish to see a nurse mourning the untimely death of another patient.

Providing quality care is the nurse's priority, and nothing may be permitted to detract from that care, certainly not the moods or the feelings of the nurse. Nursing, then, can be viewed as a show that "must go on" and, indeed, does, despite the actor's (nurse's) personal needs at the time of the performance. The audience (patient) is entitled to the best possible performance and the actor (nurse) must provide it to the best of her ability.

While nurses may be compared to actors in that both must play a role, there is a significant difference between the roleplaying of the two. Actors play one role at a time, while nurses play several simultaneously. For example, the nurse may care for six patients, each with a different problem and, therefore, a different need. One patient, like terminally ill Mrs. Olive, may require compassion and understanding in her suffering; another, like elderly, confused Mr. Hays, may need gentle caring and repeated reassurance; and yet another, like young and relatively healthy Ms. Cordrey, may need the nurse to join her in a celebration to express relief. How is it possible to be cast simultaneously in multiple roles and to play these roles effectively?

This study explores how nurses meet the needs of two mutually exclusive groups of patients: terminally ill patients in the last stages of illness and acutely ill patients expected to recover. One exploration gives rise to two pivotal questions: Are there differences in the ways nurses care for the living and the dying? Do the disparate needs of the two groups result in role conflict for the nurses caring for them?

Comparison of Terminal and Acute Care

The dying patient's psychological stress must be relieved even if "medical treatment aimed at curing him has been discontinued" (Samarel, 1988; Young & Jacobs, 1983). Care of the dying is intended not to cure the patient, but to provide comfort and freedom from pain.

The concepts of cure and care differ widely. The objective of curing is to eliminate disease; care focuses on the overall welfare of the patient and the disease experience (Benoliel, 1972). The goal of the curative therapies offered in hospitals is the prevention of death and the ultimate discharge of the patient. As the possibility of cure diminishes, however, the less aggressive, more caring aspect of attention assumes greater importance.

The difference in intention between terminal and acute care results in significant disparities in philosophies and goals. These have been described as follows by Burger (1980), Samarel (1988), and Young and Jacobs (1983).

Death as Natural versus Death as Failure. In terminal care, death is viewed as a natural termination of life and accepted as such. Rather than deny death or prolong life for dying patients, goals for care are focused on comfort in the dying process; care is palliative. Acute care, however, is designed on the premise that most patients will be discharged. Treatment in acute care is aggressive; its goal is the maintenance of life and the prevention of death.

Quality of Life as Goal versus Survival as Goal. The focus of terminal care is the quality of remaining life. For this reason, physical, psychological, and spiritual comfort is the priority of care for the dying. While comfort is certainly an important facet of acute care, the priority of care in the hospital is survival.

Multidimensional Approach to Care versus Emphasis on Physical Care. While physical comfort is a priority of terminal care, there is equal emphasis on the patient's psychological and spiritual well-being. Acute care, while certainly supporting a multidimensional approach to care, has its major emphasis on the physical care needed to maintain and support life and to prevent death.

Bereavement Care versus Care Ending at Death. Terminal care extends past the patient's death into the period of bereavement experienced by the family. In the hospital, however, care ends with the patient's death.

Family-centered Care versus Individual as Patient. Terminal care involves the patient's family. This can be observed in the extended visits encouraged of all family members, the participation by the family in the care of the patient, and the support provided to the family by clergy and the social services, as well as by doctors and nurses. Family involvement in hospitals is ordinarily peripheral, with the individual patient being the focus of care.

Most general hospital units include patients who are acutely ill and expected to recover, as well as terminally ill patients in the last stages of illness. Reconciling two conflicting modes of care within a single setting may well affect health care professionals. How do individual nurses respond to these apparently incongruous concepts of care in the course of professional practice? How do they perform their challenging task?

The Role of the Registered Nurse

Examination of the role of the registered nurse reveals several principles that apply across all areas of practice and specialization. A review of the philosophies of various programs of nursing education across the country, as revealed in self-evaluation studies prepared by nursing education programs prior to accreditation site visits, likewise demonstrates agreement on several concepts basic to nursing. These are a reverence for life, a respect for the dignity and individuality of each person, and a determination to act on beliefs. These philosophies portray the patient as a holistic being with physical, psychological, sociocultural, and spiritual dimensions. The objectives of the registered nurse with respect to patient care are achieved through effective interpersonal interactions within caring relationships with patients.

Nursing is defined by the American Nurses Association (1980) as the "diagnosis and treatment of human responses to actual or potential health problems." This broad statement encompasses older definitions of nursing that specifically refer to body, mind, and spirit (National League of Nursing Education, 1937). The concept of spirit refers to the sense of meaning and purpose, the drive toward achieving maximum potential as a human being. It may be understood within a religious, philosophic, or humanistic context (Flynn, 1980). An important emphasis of all quality nursing care is the understanding that each individual must be understood as a unified whole in constant interaction with the environment (Rogers, 1987, 1988; Roy, 1984).

To summarize, the universal view of the role of the registered nurse includes a philosophy describing the individual as holistic and multidimensional; a respect and value for life; a responsibility to assist the individual in the promotion and restoration of health, prevention of illness, and attainment of a peaceful death; and maintenance of a therapeutic environment in which to achieve these goals.

While there seems to be agreement regarding the definition of nursing and the role of the nurse, the fact remains that the needs of two separate and distinct patient populations within a single setting may require the registered nurse to change roles as she moves from one activity to another. Such transitions will result in role conflict if the role expectations are contradictory or mutually exclusive.

The nurse simultaneously fights death with the acutely ill and cares for the dying. This setting, containing two sets of disparate concepts, may render any universal view of nursing ambiguous. Do these disparate concepts result in contradictory role expectations for nurses?

A similar role conflict resulting from attempts to meet the differing needs of two patient populations is found in obstetrical nurses who care for patients experiencing induced abortions. Second-trimester abortions using hypertonic saline solution conflict with the nurses' goal of preserving life and are therefore upsetting. It has been observed that physical contact with the fetuses was particularly disturbing to obstetrical nurses because of the resemblance of the fetuses to premature infants (Baluk & O'Neill, 1980; Kaltreider, Goldsmith & Margolis, 1979). The general duty nurse, then, is not unique in dealing with conflicting roles within a single setting.

THE PROBLEM

Nursing can be viewed as subculture with distinct norms, role patterns, and ideologies. Registered nurses share similar motivational patterns, nursing philosophies, and personal values and attitudes toward life and death. These patterns, philosophies, and attitudes affect their interactions with patients. For research in the care of dying patients, see Amenta (1984), Didich and Weick (1989), Dusch (1988), Eagen (1981), Gabriel (1988), Krantzler (1982), Pannier (1980), and Williams (1982).

A hospital-based hospice is one type of unit where nurses care for both terminally and acutely ill patients. The purpose of a hospice is to provide health care and support services to terminally ill patients and their families.

While nurses may be a homogeneous group with regard to role identity, the patients in a hospital-based hospice are not. Nurses care for two distinct groups of patients in such a setting: terminally ill patients designated as "hospice" patients, and patients who are acutely ill and expected to regain their health. The reason for this dichotomy in patient profile is a matter of practicality and economics. Most units in community hospitals have a 30- to 50-bed capacity. Although a particular unit may be designated as a discrete hospice, rarely are there 30 hospice patients to fill the unit. Rather than operate under capacity, hospitals designate a limited number of beds for hospice patients, leaving the remainder for acutely ill patients. The result is a dichotomous patient population cared for by a group of hospice nurses.

Are there meaningful differences between the behaviors of nurses with terminally ill patients and the behaviors of these nurses with the acutely ill? The aim of this research is to describe and, ultimately, understand the role transition of a group of nurses considered representative or those nurses who care for the living and the dying.

METHOD

An ethnographic design was employed in this study. Nurses and patients were observed on a 35-bed unit in a community hospital in a suburban area of the northeast United States.

Definition of Terms

For purposes of this study, an acutely ill patient is defined as an individual with an acute or chronic illness, regardless of the nature or severity of the illness. This individual receives aggressive medical treatment. The patient may be a 25-year-old person with a hernia or an 85-year-old person with congestive heart failure. Patients are expected to return home and resume daily life to the optimal degree possible.

A terminally ill patient is an individual who has discontinued aggressive medical treatment designed to prolong life. These patients are traditionally referred to in hospital settings as "no codes" or "DNRs" (Do Not Resuscitate).

Guiding Questions

The questions that guided this research include the following:

1 In what ways do the interactive behaviors of nurses with terminally ill patients differ from the interactive behaviors of these nurses with acutely ill patients?
2 What is the relationship between the interactive behaviors of nurses and their expressed personal values and nursing philosophies?
3 What is the relationship between the observed and reported interactive behaviors of nurses?

Data Collection

The primary mode of data collection was participant observation. Other methods of data collection were informal interviews with nurses and demographic questionnaires, in addition to review of supporting documents such as nurses' notes, job descriptions, and staff development programs.

Data Analysis

The extensive field notes generated by the data collection were analyzed systematically using a constant comparative method of qualitative analysis within a symbolic interactionist framework. (Glaser and Strauss (1967), Hutchinson (1986), and Wilson (1986, 1989) provide detailed discussions of the grounded theory approach to qualitative research.)

Symbolic Interactionism

Symbolic interactionism focuses on the social construction of reality. An interactionist perspective maintains that individuals interpret others' actions and respond to those actions based on their interpreted meaning of them. That is, responses are constructed socially by continually interpreting the meanings of stimuli. As symbols, speech and gestures are stimuli that elicit responses from others based on their interpreted meaning. (Blumer (1969) offers a complete discussion of symbolic interactionism.)

Responses are based upon interpretations of others' acts, and interpretations are dependent upon a personal value system in combination with situational experience. For example, a nurse's personal values and attitudes toward the death experience in combination with the perceived needs of a particular patient at a given time will contribute to the nurse's interpretation of the patient's speech and gestures. This interpretation will affect the nurse's responses to the patient.

To expand upon this example, if a particular nurse is frightened at the thought of death and view death as something to be denied, she may consistently evade the issue of death. It is possible that the nurse has never had the opportunity to explore with others the idea that death may not be frightening but may be viewed as a welcomed end to a long and full life. This nurse's terminally ill patient reaches out to the nurse and states, "I am dying." The response of the nurse may be to protect the patient from the fear of the reality of impending death. The nurse states, "You seem better today," because the nurse perceives that this is what the patient needs and wants to hear. In reality, this patient may wish for acknowledgment of the impending death so that feelings may be shared.

A nurse's response may vary, too, depending on the "type" of death. For example, the death of a child may be viewed as unfair; the death of an individual who has lived a long and useful life may be accepted by the nurse; death that ends suffering and pain may be viewed as welcome.

There are many possible responses to a patient's statement, "I am dying." The response is dependent upon the respondent's interpretation of the patient's need. From a symbolic interactionist perspective, the focus is on the meanings of the symbols and acts in the interaction process. In this inquiry, interactive nursing behaviors are examined within a symbolic interactionist perspective.

Interpersonal perception, the way individuals perceive and respond to others, involves values and philosophies and is reflected in patterns of behavior. It is difficult to face others' suffering if one is unable to deal with one's own. For example, an individual afraid of his or her own death will avoid facing others' deaths. Dass and Gorman (1985) argue that to be of most service to others a person must first face personal needs and doubts. How one performs as a nurse, therefore, will depend upon one's philosophy and values.

Values are action-oriented; they give direction and meaning to one's life. Values determine what an individual does and the manner—either caring or uncaring—in which it is done.

Symbolic Interactionism and Nursing Care

Nursing is a caring process involving compassionate concern for the patient, an art, and an attitude. Caring, as a feeling that motivates action, implies commitment to serve the one cared for. Caring behaviors are interpreted through the symbols of speech and gestures. However, caring cannot be captured by a behavior or a set of behaviors, but only by the significance of acts expressing specific attitudes and meanings on the part of the actors (Noddings, 1984). The meaning and intention behind the acts distinguishes caring from uncaring behavior. To understand nursing behavior, therefore, one must conceptualize the values and philosophies that give direction to the lives of the individuals whose behavior one is observing. (A more extensive discussion of caring in nursing is offered in Appendix C.)

Within the framework of symbolic interactionism, nurses' interactions with acutely ill and terminally ill patients were compared with each other in a search for patterns. The patterns of interaction that emerged from the data fell into three categories of nursing care: physical, psychological, and spiritual. Constant comparisons revealed similarities in and differences between nursing interactions with both types of patients, generalizations with regard to overt and covert norms and behaviors, and relationships between expressive (self-reported) and instrumental (observed) domains. These findings are analyzed in Chapter 4.

This research endeavors to generate an empirically based theory of nurses' role interaction through constant comparison of the interactive behaviors of these nurses with the two groups of patients described above.

LITERATURE CITED

Amenta, M. M. (1984). Traits of hospice nurses compared with those who work in traditional settings. *Journal of Clinical Psychology, 40*(2), 414–420.

American Nurses' Association. (1980). *Nursing: A social policy statement.* Kansas City, MO: Author.

Baluk, U., & O'Neill, P. (1980). Health professionals' perception of the psychological consequences of abortion. *American Journal of Community Psychology, 8*(1), 67–75.

Benoliel, J. Q. (1972). The concept of care for a child with leukemia. *Nursing Forum, 11*(2), 194–204.

Blumer, H. (1969). *Symbolic interactionism.* Englewood Cliffs, NJ: Prentice-Hall.

Burger, S. (1980). Three approaches to patient care: Hospice, nursing homes, and hospitals. In M. Hamilton and H. Reid (Eds.), *A hospice handbook: A new way to care for the dying* (p. 132). Grand Rapids, MI: Eerdmans.

Dass, R., & Gorman, P. (1985). *How can I help?* New York: Alfred A. Knopf.

Didich, J., & Weick, J. K. (1989). The development of a palliative care program. *Cleveland Clinic Journal of Medicine, 56*(8), 762–764.

Dush, D. M. (1988). Psychological research in hospice care: Toward specificity of therapeutic mechanisms. *Hospice Journal, 4*(2), 9–36.

Eagen, M. C. (1981). The nursing functions/role implications in a free-standing hospice (Doctoral dissertation, University of Michigan, 1981). *Dissertation Abstracts International, 42,* 2437A.

Flynn, P. A. (1980). *Holistic health: The art and science of care.* Bowie, MD: Robert J. Brady.

Gabriel, R. M. (1988). Advancing the state of hospice care: A continuum of research methodologies. *Hospice Journal, 4*(3), 73–82.

Glaser, B. G., & Strauss, A. L. (1967). *The discovery of grounded theory: Strategies for qualitative research.* New York: Aldine.

Hutchinson, S. (1986). Grounded theory: The method. In P. L. Munhall & C. J. Oiler

(Eds). *Nursing research: A qualitative perspective* (pp. 111–130) Norwalk, CT: Appleton-Century-Crofts.

Kaltreider, N. B., Goldsmith, S., & Margolis, A. J. (1979). The impact of midtrimester abortion techniques on patients and staff. *American Journal of Obstetrics and Gynecology, 135*(2), 235–238.

Krantzler, N. J. (1982). Treatment for cancer: Nurses and the sociocultural context of medical care (Doctoral dissertation, University of California at Berkeley, 1982). *Dissertation Abstracts International, 44,* 212A.

National League of Nursing Education. (1937). *A curriculum guide for schools of nursing.* New York: Author.

Noddings, N. (1984). *Caring.* Berkeley: University of California Press.

Pannier, E. A. (1980). The hospice care-giver: A qualitative study (Doctoral dissertation, Northwestern University). *Dissertation Abstracts International, 41,* 2456A.

Rogers, M. E. (1987). Rogers' science of unitary human beings. In R. R. Parse, *Nursing science: Major paradigms, theories, and critiques.* Philadelphia: W. B. Saunders.

Rogers, M. E. (1988). Nursing science and art: A prospective. *Nursing Science Quarterly, 1*(3), 99–102.

Roy, C. (1984). *Introduction to nursing: An adaptation model* (2nd ed.). Englewood Cliffs, NJ: Prentice-Hall.

Samarel, N. (1988). Caring for life and death: Nursing in a hospital-based hospice (Doctoral dissertation, Rutgers University, 1987). *Dissertation Abstracts International, 48,* 2607B.

Williams, C. A. (1982). Role considerations in care of the dying patient. *Image, 14*(1), 8–11.

Wilson, H. S. (1986). Presencing—Social control of schizophrenics in an antipsychiatric community: Doing grounded theory. In P. L. Munhall & C. J. Oiler (Eds.), *Nursing research: A qualitative perspective* (p. 131–144). Norwalk, CT: Appleton-Century-Crofts.

Wilson, H. S. (1989). *Research in nursing.* Redwood City, CA: Addison-Wesley.

Young, D., & Jacobs, A. M. (1983). *Hospice nursing: A model curriculum for continuing education.* Los Angeles: California State University.

Chapter 2

Four South, the "Hospice Unit"

Madison Medical Center (MMC) is a 500-bed community hospital located in Willow Grove, a suburban town in the northeast United States. Four South at MMC is the setting in which nurses care for the living and the dying. In this chapter, the setting and the cast of Four South are introduced.

THE UNIT

Four South is known throughout MMC as the "hospice unit." According to the initial proposal for the development of Four South as a hospice unit, the goal of the unit was "to provide nursing and support services to the hospice patient and family," enabling patients to live "as fully and comfortably as possible until they die."

Getting off the elevator on the fourth floor, one exits into an alcove opposite the Four South nurses' station. This is the center of the floor. Corridors extend to the left and right (see Figure 1). Along one wall of the right corridor are stretchers, a scale, dietary rack, wheelchair, and linen hamper. This corridor, containing several patient rooms, two supply rooms, a shower and tub

11

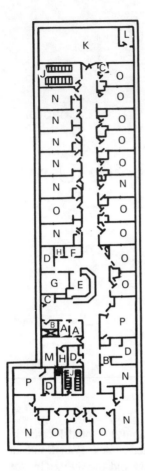

Figure 1 Four South floor plan. A, Elevator; B, Office; C, Closet; D, Storeroom; E, Nurses' station; F, Medication room; G, Nurses' lounge; H, Rest room; J, Stairs; K, Solarium; L, Family room; M, Showers; N, Semiprivate patient room; O, Private patient room; P, Patient suite.

room, closet, and water fountain, forms the stem of a T. The cap of the T also contains several patient rooms.

Including the three patient rooms opposite the nurses' station, there are 18 patient rooms on the left side of the floor. At the end of the corridor are double wooden doors leading to a large day room, windowed on three sides, with views of the river below and of the surrounding areas.

The nurses' lounge, a small windowless room situated behind the nurses' station, is used for work and for the nurses' coffee breaks and lunch.

THE PATIENTS

While Four South has a 35-bed capacity, at no time during the data collection period was the unit filled to capacity. The average daily patient census was 29, of whom between 4 and 19 were terminally ill patients. The average age of all patients on days of observation was 64 years. The average age of terminally ill patients on these days was 74 years.

Most terminally ill patients had a diagnosis of cancer in some form. A few had diagnoses unrelated to cancer such as congestive heart failure, diabetes, or cerebrovascular accident. Diagnoses for the acutely ill patients were as varied as they are on any general medical-surgical unit.

Length of stay for patients was varied and ranged from overnight to several months. Many of the terminally ill patients were continually readmitted and had established relationships with the nursing staff prior to the current admission. This continual readmission, combined with extended durations of stay for some patients, may have facilitated familiarity and intimacy between patients and staff.

A TYPICAL DAY

While no two days are exactly the same on Four South, or on any other unit for that matter, it is possible to describe a typical day, a composite description of all observation days.

The day staff begins arriving at 6:50 a.m. and all are present by seven. Coats are hung, handbags are put away in lockers, and everyone assembles at the nurses' station, ready for work. The night staff is ready to leave at this time. Occasionally, after a busy night, the night staff remains until several minutes after seven to complete their nurses' notes.

Pat, the assistant head nurse, arrives at seven with the rest of the staff. In her early forties and married with four children, Pat has been a registered nurse (RN) for five years and has worked in hospice for two of those years. She is new to Four South and to MMC, having been hired four weeks prior to the onset of data collection. While she is fair, a hard worker, and usually available to assist other nurses when needed, she states, "They [the nurses] haven't completely accepted me yet. It takes time." She adds in a confident manner, "They will."

Pat is always "in charge" when she is on duty. Her daily responsibilities as charge nurse include review of the patient census and staffing for the day, and adjustment of staff assignments based on that review. This means that she assesses the number of patients on Four South each day and the extent of nursing care required by each. She may then alter the nursing assignment schedule to divide more fairly the work among all staff present. In addition to being in charge, Pat is responsible for patient care.

Barbara, known to patients as the "head nurse," usually arrives about 8:30 or 8:45. Barbara is in her late twenties, married with no children, attractive and vivacious with an easy smile. She has been an RN for five years, the last 18 months of which have been in hospice at MMC. She appears to be consistently attentive to the expressed needs of her staff and, when unable to meet a need or a request of a particular nurse, offers a plausible explanation. The staff perceives her as helpful, hardworking, understanding, and fair.

Barbara, in reality, is an administrator. Although her office is on the unit and she wears a white nurses' uniform, her administrative duties usually prevent her from becoming involved in direct patient care. Nevertheless, Barbara is quite conscientious about making rounds on the unit every day, visiting each patient, introducing herself to newly admitted patients, and chatting briefly with them about how they feel.

Pat and Barbara are the newcomers to Four South. The remainder of the professional day staff has been on the unit from 5 to 8½ years. With the exception of Barbara and Pat, all have been present since the inception of the hospice concept at Four South five years earlier. At that time, the Four South staff was given the choice of remaining on the unit and working with terminally ill patients or being transferred to another unit within MMC. The nurses remaining made a conscious decision to work with dying patients.

In addition to Barbara and Pat, the day nursing staff consists of six RNs and two licensed practical nurses (LPNs). All Four South nurses consider themselves to be hospice nurses.

Liz is in her late fifties and has been working as a nurse for the past 12 years, the last 7½ at MMC. She is divorced with grown children. Liz's unique contribution to hospice nursing is her empathy. She maintains that this is possible because she herself experienced a mastectomy several years ago and can therefore relate to "other cancer patients." Liz speaks and moves quickly, usually making her presence known by singing quietly as she works or by muttering good-naturedly to herself. "Don't pay any attention to me," she will advise. Liz values efficiency and becomes easily flustered when she perceives a lack of efficiency in her work.

Sandy is in her mid-forties and has been in nursing for 13 years, the last 8½ at MMC. She is married and has two children. In contrast to Liz, she has a calmness about her that is manifested in her quiet and purposeful manner of speech. Amy and Sharon are in their thirties with 13 and 16 years of nursing experience. Both are married, Amy with no children and Sharon with one child. Judy and Katie, both RNs in their mid-forties, work part time.

Ellen and Kim are both LPNs. Ellen is in her late twenties, married with no children, and has worked part time for the past seven years in nursing, all at MMC. Kim is in her early thirties, divorced with one child, and has worked full time at MMC since completing her LPN training 5½ years ago. In addition to the nurses, there are four nurse's aides and two secretaries on the Four South day shift.

There is an air of friendliness on Four South. Most nurses on the day shift have been working together for more than five years and have developed deep personal relationships with one another. They speak to each other of husbands, children, in-laws, and broken washing machines as well as of day-to-day work-related issues. According to Kim, "We're more than coworkers. We're family for each other. We really care about each other."

An example of this mutual caring was demonstrated early one morning when Sandy led Liz into the nurses' lounge. Liz was protesting to Sandy in an agitated voice, "But I have so much work to do."

Sandy replied in her very soothing tones, "Now, Liz. You take it easy today. We'll all help get your work done. You just relax for a while." Sandy later explained that Liz's semiannual medical examination was scheduled for that afternoon and she was quite worried about it, as she tended to be since her mastectomy.

At 7:00 each morning Pat obtains a very brief oral report about each patient from the night charge nurse. This report consists primarily of any problems experienced by patients and is used by Pat to adjust the nursing assignments to disperse the workload more appropriately. While she is obtaining this report the nurse's aides begin to make rounds to each patient and take morning temperatures, blood pressures, and pulses for each. The RNs and LPNs, together with the night staff, complete a narcotic count required at the conclusion of each shift and check the continuous intravenous infusions on the unit.

After Pat makes final adjustments in nursing assignments and announces them to the staff, all begin their morning routine. Each nurse obtains a looseleaf medication book in which she places the medication sheets for her patients. There are four such books along with four looseleaf books containing patient care records, or cardexes. These cardexes contain all the information needed to care for a particular patient: age; diagnosis; physicians' orders for diet, treatment, activity, and diagnostic tests; list of medications ordered; and plan of nursing care. Each nurse checks both the medication and patient care cardexes and notes pertinent facts about each patient's care on a daily assignment sheet that is used as a guide for planning the day's work.

This is all done at the table in the nurses' lounge while listening to a taped report from the night shift. The report, begun at approximately 7:15, is an update on each patient's status and contains such information as patient name, room and bed, diagnosis, age, physician, treatments and diagnostic tests scheduled for that day, and patient's condition or particular problems occurring during the previous 24 hours. The nurses' aides continue to obtain patients' vital signs while the nurses listen to report.

Pat keeps a legal pad in front of her. She makes pertinent notations about each patient while listening to the taped report. She continually stops the tape as the group discusses particular patients:

I'm watching her closely—she's a very sick lady.

Did you get that urine specimen on Mr. Smith yesterday?

No. He couldn't give it to me. Look and see if they got it on nights.

Ohhhh! [a sound of disappointment that an important test had not been completed].

We need to work more with his daughter today, [speaking of the family of one of the hospice patients]. She needs a little break. She's been caring for him continuously for months. I'll speak to Sheila [the social worker on the hospice team] to see what we can set up.

Let's see about a No Code [order] for her [referring to a terminally ill patient admitted during the night]. She's really bad. She won't last long. Let's get a hospice consult today.

Yes.

He doesn't know.

Doesn't know what?

That he has cancer. That means don't tell 'em!

These are typical comments heard during the report. They serve to communicate information not found on the cardex but necessary for comprehensive nursing care.

Not all the nurses remain in the lounge during the entire report. They come and go, being sure to be present to hear reports on their own patients. Often, when the report on patients in other sections is being played, a nurse will leave to answer a patient's call light or to look something up in a patient's chart, kept in a rack in the nurses' station.

Report is usually completed by 7:45. At that time the RN for each section discusses the care of her patients with the nurses' aide or LPN working with her. The entire staff then begins direct patient care. For the RNs, this includes assessment of physical and emotional status, assistance with hygiene and activity, implementation of treatments, psychological support, and education. Regularly scheduled medications are administered at 9:00 a.m. and at 1:00 p.m., with medications for pain administered at any time, as patients need them.

While regular morning care is provided, the area around the nurses' station hums with activity. Phones ring constantly and are answered by the unit secretary or by Pat. Calls are made to arrange for transportation of patients to diagnostic testing or to obtain results of patients' diagnostic tests. Physicians ask questions about their patients, write orders in charts, and dictate discharge summaries into the dictaphone. Transporters come back and forth with patients for diagnostic testing or treatments in other areas of the hospital. Nurses make inquiries regarding the scheduling of tests or clarification of orders. Members of the hospice team are present to make rounds. The dietitian looks up a diet order on a patient chart.

Barbara, in by 8:45, receives an oral report from Pat on the status of all patients. She then makes rounds, visiting each patient. This is time consuming but, according to Barbara, "really important if I am to know what's happening on the unit."

At 9:30 the nurses' aides usually take 15 or 20 minutes for a coffee break in the lounge. The nurses take their break about 10:00 a.m. This break consists of 15 or 20 minutes in the lounge with a cup of coffee, more often than not interrupted by a call from another staff member for help with a patient. Barbara tries to support the nurses' break by helping in any way she can with patients while they are on break and by trying not to disturb them unless it is absolutely necessary.

Between 10:30 and 11:30 each nurse is either completing care and treatment of her patients or beginning to write a daily progress note (nurses' note) on each patient's chart. Lunch is taken in two separate shifts, assigned by Pat with input from each nurse and aide as to whether the early or late lunch is preferred. The first group goes to lunch from 11:30 to 12:15 and the second from 12:30 to 1:15. Following lunch, afternoon medications are administered, nurses' notes are completed, and report is taped for the evening shift.

Twice monthly hospice support meetings involve the entire staff. The purpose of the support meetings is to provide psychological support for the nurses through discussion of problems and issues and venting of feelings related to the care of terminally ill patients. According to Sheila, the social worker who leads the bimonthly meetings:

> Support group is an area in which to vent . . . about families that are wearing [the nurses] out. They become emotionally involved with some families more so than with others. Support helps them to identify the transference that is taking place and to then develop insight into their emotions. It's a place for problem solving. They can back off from some families if that is indicated and the others will cover for them. They also talk about their frustration with the profession.

Support group is sacred to Four South nurses. It is a forum where anything and everything can be freely discussed in complete confidence. Visitors, including researchers, are excluded from this group. Barbara, who holds a managerial position, is also excluded. Pat, however, is a part of the group. Sheila considers this a problem. Because Pat is a manager and is responsible for evaluating the nurses on Four South, Sheila maintains that the group meetings have not been effective since Pat joined a few months ago. She states that the nurses do not speak freely with Pat present.

> They'll never accept her. She's management. The conversation tends to be very superficial, like "How was your weekend?" After all, she does their evaluations and may remember their weaknesses shown in support when it comes time for evaluations.

Barbara maintains that Pat belongs in the group because she provides direct care to hospice patients and needs this support as much as the rest of the staff.

Although attendance at support group has been unaffected by this conflict, according to Sheila the quality of the interactions at the meetings had declined significantly.

The meeting, held on alternate Wednesday mornings from 10:30 to 11:30, means that all nursing care must be completed by 10:30. It also means that the remainder of the day is spent catching up on those things that are usually done during the meeting time. Barbara and the hospice coordinator cover the unit during the meeting.

The foregoing is a description of a typical day, but every day contains exceptions. Some days are extremely busy, with patients needing more care for pain control or with education of patients with newly diagnosed problems. On some days beds are repeatedly soiled. Often, Barbara, Pat, or other members of the nursing staff have meetings. Meetings for one staff member mean more work for others.

Chapter 3

Five Days in the World
of Four South

MONDAY

7:00 a.m.

Sharon and Liz are off today. Amy, Sandy, and Katie are sitting around the table in the nurses' lounge smoking cigarettes and drinking coffee. Each has a blank sheet of paper in front of her; they are ready to write their patient assignments for the day. While they are waiting for Pat to announce the assignments, their conversation drifts from patient to patient. The nurses who worked on the weekend discuss how Saturday and Sunday went on Four South.

Katie, RN: Judy's pain was out of control yesterday. She was supposed to be medicated around the clock, whether or not she needed it. Evidently she wasn't. I guess *someone* decided it wasn't necessary. Anyway, when I came on at 7:00, she was screaming. I rushed into her room to find her writhing. When I walked over to her, she started screaming again and clawing at me. I can't begin to tell you how I felt. It was a *horrible* experience.

Katie's voice reflected anger, but her eyes were filled with tears as she discussed the 37-year-old patient involved. Judy Palumbo was in the terminal stages of cancer and in great pain when awake. According to the doctor's orders, she was to be kept sedated at all times to insure her comfort.

Katie asks Sandy about Ms. Martin. Forty-two years old and recently diagnosed with breast cancer, Cindy Martin had a mastectomy three days earlier.

Sandy, RN: She's probably ready to talk about it now. Poor thing, she's been avoiding it all week. She's alone and it's so hard for her.

Amy, RN: Well, honey, let me know if I can help. But if we don't get started soon, it'll be a miracle if we get to do all that we have to do, leave alone talk to the patients. It seems as if we get started later and later every day. There's really no reason to waste time like this. We have work to do.

Sandy, RN: Where *is* Pat, anyway?

Katie, RN: [Looking impatiently at her watch] It's almost 7:15 and we haven't even started report. Why do we have to sit here wasting time waiting for Pat to make the assignments?

Sandy, RN: I really like to get started early. I usually don't get much of out that report, anyway. It takes forever and they [the nurses on the previous shift who taped the report] really don't tell you what you need to know. I go in and look at and feel the patient. I talk to them. I get my info that way.

Katie, RN: Who took care of Mr. Kelly this weekend?

Amy, RN: I did. He's going downhill quickly. I really don't think he'll last too long.

Katie, RN: I was afraid of that. He's been so frightened. He won't talk about it, but I'm sure he knows what's going on.

Amy, RN: You're right. He's scared stiff and denying the whole thing. He really can't face it. And, I guess, he never will. But at least we can keep him comfortable. He reminds me so much of Mr. Brent. There's another one who's denying.

Sandy, RN: I don't think so. I think he's really in touch with what's going on. It's just that he either forgets or can't communicate. Don't forget, it's his brain.

Amy, RN: You're probably right. Where *is* Pat with those assignments!

7:20

Pat finally enters the lounge with the nurses' assignments. She informs each nurse which patients she will care for and report begins. As is the usual custom, the nurses filter in and out of the lounge while the taped report is played, returning to hear the reports on their assigned patients. On more than one occasion, Pat stops the tape as the report is played to discuss particular patients.

8:05

The desk at the nurses' station is quite noisy; Four South is unusually busy today. Its elderly and very ill patients require extensive nursing care on the best of days. To add to the busyness, however, this is Monday and because many of the nurses have been off for two days they do not know the patients admitted over the weekend. In addition, the nurses must catch up on changes in the other patients' conditions. This unfamiliarity with some patients slows them down.

Amy, Sandy, Katie, and Pat are at the nurses' station checking their patients' medication orders. The call bell rings incessantly. Mr. Straus, 79 years old, terminally ill, and confused, is asking for the "supervisor" because "no one is taking care of" him.

Pat, RN: He's a real one.

Amy, RN: Let's get him transferred.

Sandy, RN: He's going to report *someone* to administration.

Amy, RN: His son told me he's always been like that and has destroyed the family.

The call bell continues to ring and Mr. Straus' voice is demanding attention.

Sandy, RN: He's not mine but I'll go in to him.

Sandy disappears down the hallway as the rest of the nurses are returning medication cardexes to their proper places and rushing off to begin their morning work.

8:30

Pat is in Mr. Straus' room helping him wash.

Mr. Straus: The nurses here forget about me. They start to wash me and then never finish.

Pat, RN: [In a matter-of-fact manner] The nurses on this floor are the best you'll find. They're very well-trained. Now wash your penis.

Mr. Straus: I don't have one.

Pat, RN: Yes you do. Now wash it.

Mr. Straus: [As he continues to wash] I can tell you about the nursing care here. It's terrible. They all watch the clock and don't care about me. I'm very sick but don't let them know it. No one rubs my back.

Pat, RN: You've done a good job [referring to Mr. Straus' washing].

Mr. Straus: Really? No one's ever said that to me before. You're a good nurse.

Pat, RN: [As she clears away the wash water] I'll be back to give you your medicine a little later.

Mr. Straus: Now don't forget!

8:50

Katie is making rounds, looking in on each patient before starting morning care. She enters Mr. Brent's room to find him sitting in bed. Mr. Brent is 62 years old and terminally ill with metastatic brain cancer. His tumor makes him forgetful and occasionally dyphasic. Mrs. Brent is sitting in a chair at the bedside. Standing in the doorway, Katie introduces herself to Mr. and Mrs. Brent.

Katie, RN: Good morning, Mr. Brent. My name is Katie and I'm your nurse today. How are you feeling?

Mr. Brent: Fine. [He looks at Katie with a puzzled expression on his face, as if she has no possible reason to ask such a question.] Do you think Father James will be around today? Oh! I forgot. It's Friday and he's not here on Fridays, is he?

Mrs. Brent: [Pointing to Mr. Brent] He's been here so often that he knows everyone's schedule.

Katie, RN: Yes, I do remember you.

Mr. Brent: [To Mrs. Brent] Now, honey. Who is that priest that comes today? Is it the woman one [referring to the hospice chaplain]?

There is more talk about the chaplain.

Mr. Brent: I've always gone to church regularly. While I'm not religious, I try. [Mr. Brent looks intently at Katie, waiting for a response.]

Katie, RN: [Changing the subject] How's your pain, Mr. Brent?

Mr. Brent: No pain. I'm great.

Katie, RN: I guess the pain medication is working. And that's why you're here.

Mr. Brent: I'm perfect. They can't find any cancer anywhere and that's why I feel good.

Mrs. Brent: [To Mr. Brent] Now, watch what you say. [Then, to Katie] He said that to the home nurse and she wrote down that he's confused and doesn't know he's sick. Now he does get confused from time to time. [She looks lovingly at Mr. Brent.] But he *does* know what's happening. What he means is that they can't find the primary site anywhere.

Mr. Brent: Not even with all the scans.

Mrs. Brent: [To Mr. Brent] So the only place they've found the cancer is in your head.

Mr. Brent: And they can't cure it.

Katie, RN: But they can control it.

Mr. Brent: Yes. You know, we have no children. That's why we get along so well. [Mr. and Mrs. Brent exchange loving glances.]

Katie, RN: [Again, changing the subject] Did you eat your breakfast?

Mr. Brent: I didn't like it.

Katie, RN: If you don't like what's on the menu you can order something else. For instance, you can always ask for fruit.

9:05

Barbara arrives and receives her report from Pat. Aware that the unit is unusually busy and that, according to Pat, the nurses are somewhat "harried," Barbara spends some time assisting them with time-consuming chores such as bedmaking and answering call bells.

Meanwhile, Katie enters Mr. Kelly's room. Mr. Kelly is 69 years old and

terminally ill with lung cancer. He is emaciated and extremely pale. His roommate, Mr. Grady, is 78 and newly diagnosed with prostate cancer.

Katie, RN: Good morning, gentlemen. How are you doing today?

Mr. Kelly: [Nods his head as if to say, "Okay."]

Mr. Grady: I didn't sleep so good.

Katie, RN: Well, how's the pain? Any problems with that?

Mr. Grady: Nope. Just tired.

Katie, RN: And how about you, Mr. Kelly? Any pain?

Mr. Kelly: No. It's been pretty good [weakly].

Katie, RN: [Looking at the breakfast trays] I see neither of you had much
for breakfast. You really should eat, you know. You really should try to eat
something. Even if you just take some fluids. I'll be back in a while to help you
wash.

Katie leaves and proceeds to Ms. Victor's room. Jackie Victor, 28, has a
fever of unknown origin.

Katie, RN: Good morning. How are you today?

Ms. Victor: Okay, I guess. Did any of the tests come back yet? I mean, did
they find out what was causing it [the fever]?

Katie, RN: Not yet. But it won't be too long now. Did you eat your breakfast [glancing at the breakfast tray]?

Ms. Victor: Not really. The smell of the stuff makes me nauseous.

Katie, RN: Well, you really should try to take some fluids. How about
some juice?

Ms. Victor: Sure.

Katie, RN: I'll bring some back with me in a while.

As Katie leaves Ms. Victor's room, she hears her name called from the
nurses' station. Helen, the Four South secretary, is hanging up the telephone as
she is calling to Katie.

Helen: [Muttering to herself] Jesus! She's [Katie] gonna have a fit when
she hears this one.

Katie, RN: [Arriving at the nurses' station] What is it, Helen?

Helen: I hate to be the one to break the news to you 'cause I know how
busy you are. But you have to go to the recovery room to pick up Mr. Nelson.
They just called and said he's ready.

Katie, RN: [More overwhelmed than angry] How am I expected to do
everything! Well, all my patients are okay for now. Would you tell Sandy to
cover for me while I go for him?

The trip from Four South to the recovery room in the main building of
MMC normally takes about five or six minutes. Katie walks quickly. She still
has much work to complete this morning. Arriving at the recovery room, the
nurse there gives Katie a report on 27-year-old Mr. Nelson's condition following his minor surgery. Then, pushing Mr. Nelson's stretcher ahead of her, Katie
begins the return trip to Four South. Because she needs to wait for an empty

elevator to accommodate the stretcher and because she is unable to move as quickly while pushing the heavy stretcher, the return trip takes Katie about 15 minutes. During this time, Katie gives her undivided attention to Mr. Nelson, discussing how he is feeling, when his intravenous will be discontinued, and the fact that Mrs. Nelson is waiting for her husband back in his room on Four South.

10:15

Barbara starts her rounds at the back end of the hall, going into every room and taking as much as five minutes with many patients. She often sits on the bed next to patients, or she stands very close to the chair in which they are sitting. This physical closeness seems to create an air of familiarity. She introduces herself to newly admitted patients, extending her hand as if to shake hands with them. When patients put a hand in hers, she continues to hold it. With her other hand, she often touches patients' arms, maintaining the contact during the entire conversation. She establishes and maintains eye contact with each patient, conveying an attitude of sincere concern and asking if there are any problems, questions, or "just anything" they want to talk about. She listens intently as they talk, her eyes reflecting genuine concern. Barbara's attention does not appear to waver during the short conversation. In a few rooms, she notices that the call bell is not within easy reach for the patient and silently moves it closer to them.

Barbara enters Mr. Auger's room. Pat had told Barbara that terminally ill Mr. Auger is refusing nursing home placement. After some talk of how the 82-year-old Mr. Auger is feeling, Barbara inquires, "How do you feel about going to the nursing home?"

Barbara attempts to discuss his feelings about this issue and then continues on her rounds.

Outside Mr. O'Hara's doorway she encounters Mrs. O'Hara, who appears quite agitated and worried. Acutely ill Mr. O'Hara is 39 years old and has had his gallbladder removed. He has been complaining of severe postoperative pain unrelieved by medication.

Mrs. O'Hara: I'm so upset. He's never been like this in 12 years of marriage. And this is the second operation he's had in a month. I'm starting to get very nervous. I don't know what to do. I'm thinking of transferring him to the city.

Barbara, RN: [Touching Mrs. O'Hara's arm and looking at her sympathetically] Well, the girls are trying to get in touch with the doctor.

Mrs. O'Hara: I know. It's not them. They've all been wonderful. And I'm sorry I'm such a pest. But . . .

Barbara, RN: [Again, touching Mrs. O'Hara's arm] Now, I'd be worried, too. I don't blame you. And the girls know that you're not blaming them. I think you're right to be concerned about your husband. After all, you don't know what's wrong with him and it's hard to see him like this. I'm going to try to call the doctor right now.

Barbara interrupts her rounds to contact Mr. O'Hara's physician. She walks to the nurses' station and attempts to have him paged. When, after several minutes, he doesn't respond to the page, Barbara calls his office. The office nurse tells Barbara that the doctor is at the hospital. Barbara again tries to page him.

After several more minutes, the page is answered and the call is returned. Barbara explains Mr. O'Hara's problem and the fact that Mrs. O'Hara is upset about her husband's pain. The physician gives Barbara an order for a stronger pain medication for Mr. O'Hara and advises that he will be in to see his patient within the hour. Barbara hangs up the phone and turns to Helen.

Barbara, RN: I'm really worried about him. The doctor says he just has a low pain tolerance. But he does seem to be in a lot of pain and there is no apparent reason for it.

Barbara proceeds to the medication room and prepares the new medication for Mr. O'Hara. She returns to Mr. O'Hara's room and gives him the medication, explaining to Mr. and Mrs. O'Hara that the physician will be in within the hour to visit.

Barbara then continues her rounds, entering Mrs. Fowler's room. Terminally ill Mrs. Fowler, 79 years old, has congestive heart failure. She is unresponsive. Barbara walks to the bed, pauses at the bedside and looks silently at Mrs. Fowler for a few moments. She gently touches Mrs. Fowler's unresponsive hand, briefly resting her own hand on Mrs. Fowler's. Then, lifting her hand from Mrs. Fowler's, she slowly brushes a few hairs from Mrs. Fowler's pale forehead. Barbara silently leaves Mrs. Fowler's room.

11:15

Katie and Amy pass each other in the hallway as they rush in opposite directions.

Amy, RN: Will you look at the time! I guess a break is too much to expect around here today.

Katie, RN: Break! Ha! I'm lucky if I even get to go to the bathroom! This place is a zoo today.

Amy, RN: I'm really hungry. If we're lucky, maybe we'll get lunch, but the way things are going, I don't know.

Katie, RN: Times like this, I almost wish I had gone into real estate. At least they can eat lunch.

12:45

Sandy and Amy are in the lounge, hurriedly sipping coffee and munching on some cold food from the tray of a patient discharged earlier in the morning. This is their lunch.

2:30

As Sandy and Amy sit in the lounge writing notes on their patients' charts, Linda Remm, the hospice coordinator, enters.

Linda, RN: I just took down the MS [morphine sulfate] drip and hung a bottle of dextrose for Mr. Taylor.

Mr. Taylor is Amy's patient. He is 76 years old, semiconscious, and imminently terminal with lung cancer. In the past few days he has become increasingly restless and apprehensive. His pain is unrelieved by injections. He is comfortable only with a continuous intravenous infusion of morphine, which has been in place for the past 24 hours. Amy is visibly upset about the discontinuance of the morphine.

Amy, RN: What! Was Dr. Sims in there?

Linda replies that Dr. Sims was present and wanted the morphine discontinued. Sandy and Amy comment in agitated tones:

Sandy, RN: Well, just wait a little while and see how uncomfortable he'll get!

Amy, RN: Dr. Sims is afraid to use the drip! [To Linda] What should I do if he becomes uncomfortable? Can I hang it?

Linda, RN: Just give me time. I'll try to get the order later. Don't worry.

Linda leaves and a conversation ensues regarding Dr. Sims's reluctance to utilize the morphine to make a terminal patient comfortable. The discussion centers on ways in which a nurse may manipulate a physician into ordering a medication for a patient and the guilt associated with such manipulation. Amy comments rhetorically:

Amy, RN: Well, does the patient benefit? That's the bottom line. You do whatever you have to do so that the patient will benefit.

Sandy agrees that nurses are, indeed, the patients' advocates and need do whatever they must to ensure that patients get the care they need and deserve. Manipulation is the means and the end justifies the means.

TUESDAY

7:25

Pat, Katie, Sandy, Liz, and Sharon are in the nurses' lounge. They are about to begin to listen to the night report.

Pat, RN: You know, Mr. Taylor died last night.

Sandy, RN: How did he go? Was he on the morphine, or what?

Pat, RN: [Looking down] No.

Sandy, RN: Well, how was he?

Pat, RN: [Still looking down] Not good. He was awake, couldn't breathe, and was terrified.

Sandy, RN: And no one could get Dr. Sims to order the morphine?

Pat, RN: [Reaching over to start the tape recorder] I really don't want to talk about it. It's just too upsetting.

Pat starts the recorder and doesn't mention Mr. Taylor again. She stops the tape when it reaches the report about a woman in her forties who had a hysterectomy two days ago.

Pat, RN: She's upset. She told nights [the night shift] that she, and this is a quote, "did not see a nurse from 10 p.m. to three a.m. and was quite uncomfortable."

Sandy, RN: I hate to take care of abdominal hysterectomies. They're potsy [slow] and whining and tend to be pampered people.

Pat, RN: I'm more sympathetic toward cancer patients.

Liz, RN: Lumbosacral spine patients are whining and manipulative; I hate 'em.

Sandy, RN: Well, maybe she really didn't see anyone. I kind of doubt that, though. She was probably dozing on and off and didn't realize when Donna looked in on her. I'll have Barbara go in and chat with her. It always makes them feel better when they feel that their complaint has reached the top and that the head nurse is going to take care of it.

Pat starts the tape again. All listen intently for a few minutes. Then,

Tape Recorder: Sally Myers . . . 28 years old with systemic lupus erythematosus.

Liz, RN: Can you believe that! [Pat stops the tape.] She's pregnant—five months—and going to the city for a therapeutic abortion. She had an abortion a couple of years ago. She's not married and has a history of lupus.

Sandy, RN: [Quietly] Yesterday she was crying her eyes out about the abortion.

Liz, RN: I can't feel sorry for her. She knows what she's doing. And, of course, she's black. Who else would be in that situation?

Sandy, RN: [Silently looks down at her paper, shifting in her chair.]

Pat again starts the tape. A few minutes later,

Tape Recorder: . . . 414 bed 2, John Steele, 72 years old with uncontrolled diabetes. A 'No Code' of Dr. Sims's.

Sandy, RN: He's been really uncomfortable.

Pat, RN: [Stops the tape recorder.]

Sandy, RN: He's got gangrene and it's real bad. I'm going to try to talk Dr. Sims into a morphine drip but it's going to be difficult. You heard what happened with Mr. Taylor yesterday.

Pat again starts the tape. When Ms. Victor's name is mentioned on the tape, Katie exclaims:

Katie, RN: Stop the tape for a minute. I had her yesterday. She's in for FUO [fever of unknown origin] but I think she has other problems that are more pressing than her fever. She's 28 and has a history of psychiatric problems. She's been real withdrawn since she's been admitted, I think on Sunday. She's a social worker so she knows what's going on but she seems so immature and demanding.

Pat, RN: Well, nights said that she insisted that Dr. Henning be called during the night because she needed more medication than was ordered for her. Upon Ms. Victor's insistence, Dr. Henning was called and ordered a placebo, which was effective in relieving her restlessness. She just needs to be spanked and told that life can be rotten and she just needs to grow up.

Pat restarts the tape.

Tape Recorder: 423. Sara Fowler. 79-year-old congestive heart failure of Dr. Watson. She's a No Code. Unresponsive.

Sharon, RN: I stopped in her room before I came in here. I don't think she's going to make it through the morning.

8:45

The report is over; everyone has completed rounds on her own patients and organized herself for the day's work. Sandy begins her patient care with 73-year-old Mrs. Archer. Terminally ill Mrs. Archer has Lou Gehrig's disease (amyotrophic lateral sclerosis). She is alert and oriented but almost completely paralyzed. Because she is unable to eat she has a gastrostomy feeding tube in place. She is able to speak, but with difficulty. She is able to use her fingers to grasp objects and, if her hand is positioned properly to turn the pages of a book. It is expected that Mrs. Archer will be discharged to home care within a week.

Sandy, RN: [Speaking slowly] Now I'm going to crush these pills and feed them to you with your feeding. You can't swallow them and this is really the same. It's an easy way to take them. Now why don't you hold this for a moment [handing Mrs. Archer the syringe attached to the feeding tube] while I start the feeding?

Mrs. Archer: [Slowly and laboriously, concentrating on each word] Who . . . will . . . do . . . this . . . at home? How . . . to . . . manage?

Sandy, RN: [Taking the syringe back from Mrs. Archer] I'll arrange for nurses at home. I'll call social service and the visiting nurse service. You *will* go home with the proper help. People do go home from here, you know. I'll be back in a little while after the feeding is done. Then we can get you bathed.

Sandy walks quickly from Mrs. Archer's room and enters the next room. Mr. Young is 67 years old, ambulatory and alert, with a diagnosis of bladder tumors. Sandy brings Mr. Young his medications.

Sandy, RN: [While handing the cup of medications to Mr. Young] How are you feeling today?

Mr. Young: Not so hot. I'm pretty nauseated. Been feeling like that since I started on this new pill. [He picks a green pill from the many in the medication cup.]

Sandy, RN: When did the nausea start?

Mr. Young: I was fine until a couple of hours after I took this. Then I really couldn't even stand to eat or drink anything.

Sandy, RN: Well, you know, it *is* possible that this is making you nauseous. It is one of the side effects and some people just can't tolerate it.

*Mr. Young:*Well, I really would rather not take it again. [Places the pill back in the medication cup.] I'm really afraid that I'll throw up. And I feel so awful.

Sandy, RN: You know what I'm going to do? Watch this. I'm taking the pill with my fingers and getting rid of it. I'll check with your doctor to get something else for you.

Sandy waits until Mr. Young takes the rest of his medications, helps him to the bathroom, and leaves him while he washes. She returns to Mrs. Archer's room just as the gastrostomy feeding is completed.

Sandy, RN: Well, I see breakfast is finished! Let's get rid of this [tubing] and get you cleaned up.

Mrs. Archer: [Slowly, with concentration] That'll . . . feel . . . good. . . . Today's . . . my . . . birthday, . . . you . . . know.

Sandy, RN: Really, How old are you?

Mrs. Archer: Who . . . remembers? . . . Who . . . cares! [Laughs.]

Sandy, RN: Well, happy birthday!

Sandy, RN: [Begins assembling the basin and wash water for Mrs. Archer.] How's Iris doing with her new baby?

While Sandy bathes Mrs. Archer, the two chat about Mrs. Archer's family and about the condition of her skin, an important issue since Mrs. Archer is immobile and prone to skin breakdown.

9:15

One of Sandy's patients, a 57-year-old acutely ill woman, is becoming dizzy. Sandy is at the woman's bedside in a room at the end of the hall. She is taking her pulse and blood pressure. Using the intercom at the bedside, Sandy is speaking to Amy, who is at the nurses' station. Amy is relaying information from Sandy to the patient's physician, who has gone into the restroom at the nurses' station to wash his hands.

Sandy, RN: [On intercom] BP [blood pressure] 130/50.

Amy, RN: [To Dr. Henning] BP 130/50.

Dr. Henning: [From restroom] Okay.

Sandy, RN: BP 130/50 and [the patient is] getting nauseous.

Amy, RN: [Sounding stressed] BP 130/50 and getting nauseous . . . BP 130/50 . . . BP 130/50 and she's getting nauseous.

Dr. Henning: Okay. Okay. I heard you. You don't have to tell me six times. [He emerges from the restroom drying his hands.] She's stable and you need to calm down. I'm attending to her and she'll be fine.

Dr. Henning walks briskly toward the patient's room. The patient was fine.

9:30

Pat is standing at the nurses' station when Ms. Victor approaches. Dr. Henning has just visited her and has written new orders.

Ms. Victor: [Speaking to Pat in an emotionless voice] Dr. Henning said I can have a regular diet now.

Pat, RN: What do you want [for breakfast]?

Ms. Victor: What do they have?

Pat, RN: Anything. Tell me what you want and I'll tell the dietitian. That's the fastest way of getting a tray.

Pat and Ms. Victor continue to discuss breakfast; Ms. Victor avoids eye contact with Pat.

Pat, RN: Why don't we take a walk to the solarium so we can speak in peace without the crazy phones and everything else around here. [She gestures toward the nurses' station.]

Pat places her arm around Ms. Victor's shoulders and they walk down the hallway together toward the solarium.

Sharon, carrying an armful of clean linen, enters Mrs. Fowler's room. Sharon gives complete morning care to Mrs. Fowler omitting no aspect of her physical care. She provides exceptional skin care, carefully inspecting Mrs. Fowler for any signs of breakdown and massaging all bony prominences with lotion. Mrs. Fowler remains unresponsive throughout, moaning occasionally as Sharon, with my help, gently repositions her.

Sharon, RN: [In a directive tone] Let's be real quick so we can get her off her back. It's much harder for her to breathe on her back.

Sharon leaves the room when Mrs. Fowler is positioned comfortably and resting quietly. No verbal interaction between Sharon and Mrs. Fowler occurred during the 25-minute procedure.

10:15

Pat and Sandy are at the table in the nurses' lounge, sipping coffee. In front of each of them is an open patient chart. Each has her pen poised, as if to write in the chart. They are engrossed in conversation. Pat is telling Sandy about her walk to the solarium with Ms. Victor and the resultant conversation.

Pat, RN: So then I asked her how things were going for her. She really opened up. We talked for awhile about this relationship with this guy. It's a relationship that she really wants to terminate but is afraid to. I supported her decision to end the relationship. And then I gave her a big hug. That's important. That's the most important thing. Everyone needs that. And I told her that what she is trying to do is to get her personal life in perfect order the same way as her professional life. If I expected my personal life to be in the same order as my professional life, I'd be in trouble. You can't do that with your personal life. You just have to take what comes. I told her that. But the hug is what's important.

Sandy, RN: I'm glad you did that, Pat.

Sharon enters the nurses' lounge and fixes a cup of coffee. She takes a seat at table with Sandy and Pat.

Sandy, RN: How's Mrs. Fowler doing?

Sharon, RN: She's still breathing. I don't know why. She's still hanging on. In my head I really think she's comfortable, but I still have the feeling here [placing one hand over her heart] that she might be suffering. I guess I'm not sure what I mean. I keep going into her room to check on her. You know, to see if she's still breathing. I don't expect her to keep on too much longer. It's really dragging out for her.

Pat, RN: I didn't expect her to be here when I got in this morning.

Liz, RN: [Enters the nurses' lounge carrying a patient chart and takes a seat at the table with the others.] Well, my washing machine finally had it. Of course, it decided to break down in the middle of a full load of laundry. But that's always the way it happens, isn't it?

Sandy, RN: That machine's so old. You were expecting this to happen anyway.

Liz, RN: But who wants to go through the expense of buying another one right now?

Pat, RN: And they're expensive. I had to replace mine last year.

Liz, RN: Tell me about it! And I have so many other expenses coming up. I guess I'll go this afternoon after work. I think there's a sale at Richie's.

Pat, RN: That's where I got mine.

Sharon, RN: Boy, Liz! You've really been getting hit haven't you? First it was your roof. Then you needed a new car muffler. And now the washing machine. I hope this is it for you.

Liz, RN: You and I both! But I'll take these problems over some others that I see around here. I'm not complaining, not a lot, anyway. [She laughs.]

Sandy, RN: Every time I think of Cindy Martin, I get so angry.

Sharon, RN: What d'ya mean?

Sandy, RN: She could have gone to someone who could do a needle biopsy and then had a lumpectomy. And then she could have had radiation. Or else she could have gone to a breast surgeon, but not a general surgeon. I really couldn't ask her any of those questions because you really have to be careful. Dr. Norman is a prima donna. It wouldn't work out too well if he found out you were asking his patient those kinds of questions.

Sharon, RN: And, anyway, she's already had what she's had. No point in bringing it up now. And we really don't know if something else would have been better for her. Do we?

Sandy, RN: No. I guess not. I spent a lot of time talking with her. She's a secretary, lives alone, is very independent. She has a brother with whom she's lost touch, but no other family. Only a few close friends who she depends on for moral support.

Pat, RN: Gee, it's good you found all this out. Why don't you see what kind of support you can line up for her when she gets home. She'll need all the help she can get. Meanwhile, I need to get back out there. Barbara wants to go over the time schedule with me.

Sandy, RN: [Getting up] And I have to get going also. Pat, put me on early lunch, will you? I'm starved!

10:45

As Sandy leaves the nurses' lounge, Dr. Norman arrives on Four South.

Dr. Norman: Sandy, would you come into Ms. Martin's room with me and give me a hand. I need to remove the [surgical] drain [from her mastectomy].

Sandy, RN: Go on ahead. I'll get a suture removal set and meet you in her room.

Dr. Norman walks off toward Ms. Martin's room. Sandy arrives in the room a few moments later to find Dr. Norman at Ms. Martin's bedside speaking with her. He explains to Ms. Martin that she may feel some pain or discomfort during the brief procedure.

Sandy, RN: [Arriving at the bedside] You can hold my hand.

Sandy's hand is taken by the patient and held tightly for the duration of the procedure, about two or three minutes. Ms. Martin cries out in pain briefly and keeps her head turned away from the wound, refusing to look at it.

Dr. Norman: I'm placing a small dressing over the operative site. It's okay if you don't want to look at it yet.

Ms. Martin: I can't. I'm not ready yet.

Dr. Norman spends 15 minutes with Ms. Martin, explaining the exercises she is to do with her affected arm, discussing a prosthesis fitting, reinforcing the fact that she had a malignancy, and talking about discharge plans. Sandy remains present. When Dr. Norman leaves the room, Ms. Martin speaks to Sandy.

Ms. Martin: I thought I was gonna cry when he took off the dressing.

Sandy, RN: How do you feel now that he spoke to you?

Ms. Martin: Relieved. At least now I know for sure.

She starts to cry. Sandy immediately presses the call bell and asks Helen to send Liz into the room. Sandy later explains that she believed that Ms. Martin needed psychological support and thought that Liz was the best person to offer it because she, too, had had a mastectomy and could relate to Ms. Martin's feelings.

Liz is aware of Cindy Martin's situation and, when Helen calls her she immediately interrupts her paperwork and hurries down the hall to the room where Sandy and her patient are waiting. Liz enters the room to find Ms. Martin tearfully telling Sandy that she will never accept the mastectomy. Sandy, too, is crying. Liz, in a very brisk and officious manner, barrels her way across the room to the table where Sandy and Ms. Martin are crying and, without a word, removes her own breast prosthesis and tosses it on the table where it bounces and lands directly in front of Ms. Martin!

With that, all three women burst into laughter. Ms. Martin comments that she was unaware of the fact that Liz had also had a mastectomy. Liz shows Ms. Martin her scar, tells her how she felt when she had the surgery and how she had coped. She supports Ms. Martin's crying by saying that it is natural and healthy for her to cry. Ms. Martin states that Liz seemed to have it all together regarding the surgery.

Liz, RN: Why shouldn't I? I'm in God's hands. I know God is going to take good care of you. After all, He's taking good care of me.

Ms. Martin: Yes, I see that [weeping softly, but with an air of relief].

11:30
Katie walks into Mr. Brent's room.

Katie, RN: How are things going for you today? Where is Mrs. Brent?

Mr. Brent: Oh, she'll be up later. She had to go to the bank this morning. Now that I'm here more and more often, she has so much to do. I think this whole thing is pretty rough on her.

Katie, RN: Rough on her? [She sits in the chair next to Mr. Brent.]

Mr. Brent: Well, you know. She's worried about me. She tries not to let on about it, but I can tell. I think that's probably the hardest part for me.

Katie, RN: You mean being concerned about how she's doing?

Mr. Brent: Yes, yes. That's it. If I knew she was okay, it'd be so much easier for me. But we're pretty much alone. We really don't have anyone but each other.

Katie, RN: That must be really difficult for you. You love each other very much.

Mr. Brent: [Tears welling up in his eyes, looking down.]

Katie, RN: Have you told her?

Mr. Brent: Told her what?

Katie, RN: That you love her. And that you want to discuss her well-being.

Mr. Brent: Those things are really hard to say. And, anyway, she knows how I feel about her. She knows how much I love her.

Katie, RN: [Gently] Yes, I'm sure she does. But I believe you will both feel a lot better if you talk about those things. It's really important, you know. I understand that it's really hard to say some things, especially when you are not accustomed to. But I think you will both feel a whole lot better if you talk to each other about what is going on and about how you are feeling.

Mr. Brent: I'll give it some thought. Maybe you can help me. It's really so hard.

Katie, RN: [Reaching over and taking Mr. Brent's hand in her own] I'll try to be here for you. Let me know when you need me.

Katie gently slips her hand from Mr. Brent's, rises from chair, and leaves the room. When out of Mr. Brent's sight, she wipes a tear from her eye and continues down the hallway to Mr. Kelly's room.

Katie enters Mr. Kelly's room. He is awake, lethargic, and looks ashen. Katie gently and quickly bathes him and changes the bed linen, explaining what she is doing and confirming his comfort with each position change. When Katie is finished, Mr. Kelly looks exhausted and is breathing with some difficulty.

Katie, RN: I know that you're tired. We worked really hard, didn't we? I'll turn up the oxygen a bit until you're breathing a little better. [She reaches for the oxygen control knob on the wall above the bed.]

Mr. Kelly: [Nods his head weakly, unable to speak.]

Katie, RN: I'll be back in a few minutes to check on you.

Mr. Kelly: [Breathing heavily; nods again.]

Katie leaves the room with an armful of soiled linen for the dirty linen cart. As she stuffs Mr. Kelly's soiled linen into the cart, Pat walks by.

Katie, RN: Boy! Mr. Kelly is really going downhill fast. I don't think he'll last too much longer. Certainly not until the weekend. It's getting so hard for him to breathe. I felt guilty just washing him!

Pat, RN: Yes, I saw him this morning. It'll be a blessing if he does go quickly. It's awful not be able to breathe.

At that moment, Ms. Victor walks up to Pat and announces that she had just called the man with whom she was involved and told him that the relationship had to end. Smiling broadly, she states that it wasn't really as hard as she had anticipated. This is the first time since admission several days earlier that Ms. Victor smiles. Pat hugs her, smiles, and says, "Way to go!" Still smiling, Ms. Victor walks to her room.

Pat enters Mrs. Andrews' room and makes her bed. She works in silence. Mrs. Andrews, who is terminally ill with diabetes mellitus and a cerebrovascular accident, remains unresponsive.

1:15

Liz is in Ms. Myers' room. Ms. Myers has just recently decided to abort her pregnancy. She is single and is acutely ill with lupus.

Ms. Myers: [Crying] It's so hard to know if I'm doing the right thing. But I just can't go through and have the baby. I do want the abortion. I mean, I've given it a lot of thought and it's the best thing for me to do. But, even so, I feel awful about it.

Liz, RN: [Pauses momentarily, then walks across the room to Ms. Myers and takes her hand.] Sure you do, honey. This is not an easy thing to do. I know just what you're going through. But, no matter how much you know it's the right thing, it's still hard. I don't blame you for crying. [She places her arm around Ms. Myers' shoulders.]

1:40

Sandy emerges from the nurses' lounge with a small gift-wrapped box.

Sandy, RN: [To everyone at the nurses' station] Let's get together and bring this into Mrs. Archer's room. It's her birthday, you know, and we're going to celebrate!

Helen: I got a cake from dietary. I just need to put the candles on it. Wait for me.

Several nurses file down the hall toward Mrs. Archer's room.

2:05

Katie is sitting at the counter at the nurses' station writing her notes. Mr. Brent's call light goes on. Katie, seeing the light, immediately closes the chart on which she is writing and walks down the hallway to Mr. Brent's room. Upon entering the room, she sees Mr. and Mrs. Brent seated next to each other at the window, looking out at the river.

Mr. Brent: Oh, Katie. I hope I wasn't disturbing you. But I wanted to thank you for talking with me this morning. [Turning to Mrs. Brent] Katie and I had quite a conversation this morning, didn't we Katie? [He turns back to Katie and looks searchingly at her.]

Katie, RN: Yes, we did. Mr. Brent was talking about how difficult this whole thing is for both of you. And about how much he cares for you. Isn't that so?

Mr. Brent: [Looking down] Sometimes it's so hard to talk about the things that matter most [tears rolling down his cheek].

Mrs. Brent: [Takes a tissue from her purse and clutches it in her lap.]

Mr. Brent: Talking with Katie today made me realize how much I really love you. I think that's probably the hardest part of this whole thing.

Mrs. Brent: [Gets up from her chair and kneels in front of Mr. Brent, taking both his hands in hers, looks up at him silently.]

Mr. Brent: Oh, God. [He begins weeping.]

Mrs. Brent: [Rests her head in his lap and places her arms around his hips, weeping.]

Mr. Brent: [Places his hands gently on Mrs. Brent's hair] I do love you, you know.

Katie silently leaves the room.

WEDNESDAY

7:45

Report is finished. Katie, Sandy, Amy, Pat, Liz, and Sharon remain around the table in the nurses' lounge sipping their coffee. All full-time staff are present today, as they are every Wednesday. This scheduling makes it possible for all staff to attend the bimonthly support group and other meetings throughout the hospital. The nurses' discussion centers around several of the "problem" patients.

Katie, RN: Mr. Kelly is slipping quickly. His respirations are gurgling. I'm really concerned about Mrs. Kelly. It's been a long haul for her. She's here almost constantly. She said she doesn't want him to be alone and requested a private duty [nurse]. They really can't do anything for him and she can't afford it. I told her that wasn't really necessary and that one of us would be with him most of the time. Just so she knows that he's not alone and she can go back and forth from home. But a private duty's not really necessary. She doesn't have the money to pay for a private duty and her insurance won't cover it.

Liz, RN: And let her save her resources. Lord knows she'll be needing the money after and it doesn't pay for her to spend it on a private duty when we can be with him. Peggy [a nurses' aide] said she would be in and out during report and I'll be there when we're done. By the time we need to go to support, Mrs. Kelly will be in.

Pat, RN: You're absolutely right. No need to spend her money on a private duty. We can help with that. And I don't think it will be too many days longer now—I give him two or three at the most. Katie, just let me know how you stand and if you need any help. I'm not taking any patients today and I can free you up to be with Mr. Kelly, or I can be with him while you're busy. Just let me know.

Katie, RN: Thanks. I think I'll go and get started now. [She gathers her papers and coffee cup and leaves the room.]

Sandy, RN: I'm worried about Cindy Martin. You know, she's supposed to go home today or tomorrow and I really don't think she's ready since she lives alone and has no support system. She's still unable to look at her mastectomy and was teary when talking about it yesterday.

Amy, RN: Well, how does she feel about going home?

Sandy, RN: I spoke to her yesterday afternoon. She'd love to stay. I'm going to talk to Dr. Norman about a social service consult and maybe a home health aide for a couple of hours a week. Then, if she has to go home, at least she'll have help.

Pat, RN: Good idea!

Amy, RN: How's Mr. Steele doing?

Pat, RN: He's been extremely uncomfortable. Dr. Sims won't order the morphine drip.

Liz, RN: What's he so afraid of?

Amy, RN: I had the same problem with him on Monday. He discontinued the drip for Mr. Taylor, even though he really needed it. He's really afraid to use the morphine drip. He thinks he's supposed to wait until the very last minute. The only thing is that usually the patient goes before he decides it's the "last minute" and the wind up is that the patient is uncomfortable.

Sharon, RN: I think that's probably because he's new. He'll learn. Today's support isn't it?

Amy, RN: It sure is! And, boy, do I ever need it!

Sandy, RN: I'd kill to get to my support. I really think that's what keeps me sane around here.

Amy, RN: Well, come on! If we don't get started soon, we'll never get to support.

The nurses gather their belongings and file out of the lounge. Sandy returns to the lounge where Pat is still sitting.

Sandy, RN: Peggy is in the bathroom crying her eyes out.

Pat, RN: What's wrong?

Sandy, RN: Mrs. Downey insulted her by saying she smelled.

Peggy is a dark-skinned Hispanic and very sensitive. The staff immediately became angered at Mrs. Downey, who is elderly and confused at times. Sandy told Pat that Pat would have to do something about Mrs. Downey.

Pat leaves the lounge and knocks on the bathroom door. The door opens and a tearful, red-eyed Peggy emerges. Pat leads her into the utility room to discuss what happened. When the two emerge, Peggy looks calm. Pat then proceeds into Mrs. Downey's room to try to discuss what happened. A few moments later, she returns to the nurses' station, where the rest of the staff is waiting.

Pat, RN: I think that Mrs. Downey is mentally ill because she repeated to me what she said to Peggy and didn't see anything wrong with it. She didn't understand why Peggy was upset.

It was decided that allowances would have to be made by the staff for Mrs. Downey's senility. Peggy, however, would not be required to care for Mrs. Downey, nor have any contact with her. All seemed satisfied with that.

9:15

Mr. Steele is unresponsive and moans continuously. Peggy is in his room beginning his bed bath. Sandy walks to the bedside and works with Peggy. As they bathe Mr. Steele, Sandy and Peggy work gently, quickly, and silently, speaking neither to Mr. Steele nor to each other. After several minutes of working in silence, Sandy comments to Peggy that she does not understand why Mr. Steele is moaning, as she medicated him only 30 minutes earlier. When his care is completed, Sandy and Peggy reposition Mr. Steele on his side; he stops moaning. Peggy leaves the room. Before Sandy leaves Mr. Steele's room, she pats him on the head and asks, "There now; isn't that more comfortable for you?" Mr. Steele does not answer.

9:45

Dr. Norman is at the nurses' station looking at Ms. Martin's chart prior to his visit to her. Helen, aware that Sandy wishes to speak with Dr. Norman about Ms. Martin's discharge, hurries to the room where Sandy is working.

Helen: [In a quietly urgent tone] Come on now. Dr. Norman's here.

Sandy stops what she is doing and quickly approaches the nurses' station where Dr. Norman is standing with the chart.

Sandy, RN: Dr. Norman, could we get a social service consult for Ms. Martin?

Dr. Norman: No! She doesn't need social service. She has enough money to pay for help if she needs it.

Sandy, RN: I thought maybe they could help her get a home health aide. She lives all alone, you know.

Dr. Norman: Well, she can pick up the phone book and call any home health agency.

Sandy looks as if she has been slapped. She walks with Dr. Norman to Ms. Martin's room.

Dr. Norman: Well, hello! Let's take a look at this so we can get home now.

Dr. Norman takes off the dressing and examines the suture line while giving Ms. Martin her discharge instructions. Sandy is silent until she notices that Ms. Martin is wearing a sanitary belt.

Sandy, RN: Do you have your period?

Ms. Martin: I got it last night.

Sandy, RN: Just what you need now.

Dr. Norman: Is it heavy?

Ms. Martin: No. Not yet. But it will be. You know the way I bleed.

Dr. Norman ignores this comment and tells Ms. Martin to continue her exercises, to look for any changes at the operative site (which Ms. Martin still has consciously avoided looking at), to keep away from her dog so she does not get an infection, not do anything heavy like housework or driving, and to take a multivitamin and iron pills. He asks her if she thinks she will need help at home.

Ms. Martin: Well, I have some good friends. I'll just call them.

Dr. Norman: If you need help in the house, you can call any of the home health agencies that are in the phone book. Where do you live? You don't live in Madison County, do you?

Ms. Martin: Yes, I do. I can call Madison Visiting Nurses.

Dr. Norman: And they can get you a home health aide if you feel you need one. (This is incorrect. Madison Visiting Nurses can only intervene if they have an order from a physician. They cannot send a home health aide without first sending a nurse to the home to evaluate the patient's needs. The visiting nurse must then continue to supervise the home health aide.)

When Dr. Norman is finished with Ms. Martin, he and Sandy walk back to the nurses' station. Sandy attempts to be tactful and asks Dr. Norman for an order for a visiting nurse evaluation.

Dr. Norman: [Angrily] Why are you pushing this for her?

Sandy, RN: Well, she's going home by herself . . .

Dr. Norman: [Interrupts] I was just in there and she said she'd like to think about it. She can take care of herself. It's a pain in the neck to fill out all those consultation forms for social service. I want to do it my way.

Sandy walks off, visibly upset. She seeks Barbara and, shaking, tells her what transpired.

Sandy, RN: He's just too lazy to fill out the forms. When he said "I want to do it my way," that was it!

Barbara, RN: What's the problem?

Sandy, RN: He's sending her home alone. She hasn't even looked at her mastectomy yet and she's supposed to assess it for changes. She's anemic, taking iron, and just got her period. She has a history of hemorrhaging and is taking hormones for that. And he's sending her home alone. He thinks Reach for Recovery [a volunteer organization for women who have had mastectomies] can take care of everything. I asked Elaine [the hospice social worker] about it and she said she can't do anything without an order and that I'd better watch what I say to him because he's a prima donna and he'll turn on you in a second.

Barbara, RN: Do you want me to speak to him?

Sandy, RN: No. He'd explode. And I'd get written up—again.

Barbara, RN: Well, you did the right thing. And I wouldn't want you to be discouraged from doing this kind of thing again. And I'll support you in this if it would ever come to that. I'd go right to administration for you. [She puts her arm around Sandy's shoulders.]

Sandy, RN: Boy, am I ever striking out today!

Helen: [Standing near the two and listening to the end of their conversation] No you aren't. At least you didn't get written up! (Sandy has had run-ins with physicians before and has been "written up" for standing up for patient's rights.)

They laugh.

9:55

Katie is in Mr. Kelly's room, preparing to begin his morning care. Although Mr. Kelly has a morphine drip, he is still restless. As Katie stands at Mr. Kelly's bedside, Dr. Mitchell, an attending oncologist at MMC, walks into the room.

Katie, RN: He's restless, even with the drip. Can I give him something to calm him down?

Dr. Mitchell: Let's give him Thorazine. [He writes the order for the sedative.]

Katie, RN: Thanks.

Dr. Mitchell: Has Mrs. Kelly been in yet?

Katie, RN: Not yet. She wanted private duty nurses, but we really don't think it's necessary.

Dr. Mitchell: I agree. Let's just support them both. It won't be too much longer. [He sighs as he leaves the room.]

Katie leaves Mr. Kelly's room behind Dr. Mitchell and proceeds to the medication room to prepare the Thorazine. She returns to Mr. Kelly's room and administers it. Just as she finishes administering the medication, Mrs. Kelly arrives and, seeing Mr. Kelly tossing in his bed, becomes upset and begins to cry. Katie places her arm around Mrs. Kelly's shoulders and leads her out of the room into the hallway.

Mrs. Kelly: [Now sobbing] What can I do for him? Maybe if we got special nurses?

Katie, RN: [Gently, quietly, and with her arm still around Mrs. Kelly's shoulders] I just medicated him. He'll be comfortable in a few minutes. And the breathing is noisy, but it sounds worse to you than it really is to him. I spoke to Dr. Mitchell about private duty nurses and we both agree that it really isn't necessary. We'll be with him. He won't be alone.

Mrs. Kelly: [Relieved] I only have Blue Cross and Medicare, you know.

Katie, RN: I'm going to wait a few minutes until the medication takes effect and then I'll go in and wash him up. Why don't you have a cup of coffee in the meanwhile and I'll call you when I'm done?

Mrs. Kelly: [Placing the tissue back in her purse] Okay.

Mrs. Kelly walks down the hallway and Katie returns to Mr. Kelly's room.

10:30 to 11:30

Katie, Sandy, Amy, Pat, Sharon, and Liz leave Four South to attend their support group meeting. Helen and the nurse's aides also attend the meeting. Prior to leaving the unit, the staff completes the morning care and medications for all patients and assures their comfort. Barbara and Linda Remm, the nurse who is the Hospice Team Coordinator, cover the unit, answering the telephones, attending to call lights, and generally meeting patient needs that arise during the support meeting.

11:35

Mr. Moss, 67 years old, has diabetes. Liz enters Mr. Moss's room with a syringe of insulin and speaks with him as she administers the injection.

Liz, RN: Do you give your own insulin [at home]?

Mr. Moss: No, I've never had to.

Liz, RN: Then I'll come back later and give you the whole spiel.

Liz does not have the opportunity to return to Mr. Moss to teach insulin self-administration. Later in the day, as Liz passes Mr. Moss's room, Mr. Moss calls out to Liz from where he is sitting in his room.

Mr. Moss: Could you take my temperature—I mean my blood pressure? I feel woozy.

Liz continues walking toward the nurses' station as she calls back an answer, reading from her assignment sheet where she recorded Mr. Moss's vital signs.

Liz, RN: Let's see. Your blood pressure this morning was 160/82. It's okay.

At this point, Liz arrives at the nurses' station and busies herself with a task unrelated to Mr. Moss.

11:45

Sandy is in a patient's room administering medications. The woman is 34 years old and recently had abdominal surgery for removal of an ovarian cyst. Sandy is standing at the foot of the bed, speaking with a smile on her face, maintaining eye contact with the patient, and gently touching her foot. She asks about her bowels, promises to check the laxative order, and discusses discharge instructions. Then, she prepares to change the surgical dressing. While changing the dressing, Sandy explains exactly what she is doing.

Sandy, RN: [Pointing to the suture line] Will you look at that! That's a real beauty.

Patient: [Laughingly] How can something like that be a beauty?

Sandy, RN: You should see some of them. This is so neat. You'll hardly be able to see it when it heals.

When Sandy is finished with the dressing, she proceeds toward her next room. As she passes the elevator a small, hunched, elderly man walks off. He and Sandy greet each other warmly, she placing a kiss tenderly on his forehead. Mr. Salmon, husband of a terminally ill patient, has tears in his eyes as Sandy puts her arm around his shoulder and supports him as they walk down the hall together.

Mr. Salmon: I'm so sad. She won't make it, will she?

Sandy, RN: [Tenderly] I don't think so. Who's taking care of you at home?

Mr. Salmon: I'm taking care of myself.

Sandy, RN: Are you eating?

Mr. Salmon: I went to Perkins Pancake House last night, but I have no appetite.

Sandy, RN: You've got to force yourself. I know this is a very difficult time for you. We're here for you if you need us.

Mr. Salmon goes into his wife's room to visit and Sandy continues to the next patient's room.

12:00

Pat is involved with another patient when Dr. Sims arrives on the unit to visit Mr. Steele. Pat, hearing Dr. Sims's voice, immediately interrupts what she is doing and approaches Dr. Sims in the hallway.

Pat, RN: Would you consider a morphine drip for Mr. Steele?

Dr. Sims: [Continuing down the hallway at a rapid pace, sounding rushed as he responds to Pat.] He's that bad?

Pat, RN: Yes. He's been moaning throughout the night. And he's been medicated every four hours on the nose.

Dr. Sims: Well, let me think about it. He rushes off.

Pat, RN: [In a whisper to Sandy, who had approached the two] At least I planted the seed.

1:00

Mr. Brent is in a wheelchair at the nurses' station, waiting to be discharged. Mrs. Brent is standing beside him.

Mr. Brent: Where's my girl?

Katie, RN: [Walking down the hall toward Mr. Brent] Here I am. You don't think you can get away without saying good-bye to me, do you?

Mr. Brent: [Becoming serious] How can we thank you?

Katie, RN: For what?

Mr. Brent: You helped me to realize how important it is to say things, like
. . .

Katie bends over the wheelchair and hugs Mr. Brent. His face is buried in her shoulder, muffling the rest of his sentence and his sobs. Katie continues to hold Mr. Brent for two or three minutes until he is calm. Then, she gently releases him and wipes away his tears with a tissue produced from her pocket. Mrs. Brent puts her arms around Katie in a brief hug, releases her quickly, and blinks back her tears. Katie, too, is teary.

Katie, RN: You're both very special people. Please take care of each other. And please keep in touch.

Katie and the rest of the staff say their good-byes to the Brents as Peggy wheels Mr. Brent into the waiting elevator. The doors close and the Brents are gone. Katie, tissue in hand, walks into the lounge and sinks into a chair. Amy follows her.

Katie, RN: Some are harder than others [She sighs.]

Amy, RN: Yes, they are.

2:00
Amy is in Mrs. Pizzo's room, her arm around Mrs. Pizzo's shoulders as she assists her into the bathroom. Mrs. Pizzo is 64 years old, alert and oriented after recently having major abdominal surgery. Mrs. Pizzo eructates rather loudly, something that is normal and expected following abdominal surgery. Amy smiles with her entire face, showing genuine concern, and exclaims, "That was right from your toes!"

While Amy is is in the bathroom with Mrs. Pizzo, she maintains eye contact while listening to every word of Mrs. Pizzo's with a most interested expression on her face. Mrs. Pizzo is describing her bowel movement in great detail.

As Amy assists Mrs. Pizzo back to bed, her roommate, Mrs. Zeller, motions to Amy for assistance. Mrs. Zeller is 81 years old and recovering from a skin graft. She is oriented but screams almost constantly as if in pain. Amy approaches Mrs. Zeller's bed.

Mrs. Zeller: Do you mind if I scream?

Amy, RN: Why do you want to scream?

Mrs. Zeller: Because. [She proceeds to shriek loudly.]

Amy, RN: Stop that [firmly].

Mrs. Zeller: Well, I have to use the commode.

Amy assists Mrs. Zeller onto the commode, hands her the call bell, instructs her to ring when she is finished, and begins to leave the room. Just then, Mrs. Zeller lets out an earth-shattering shriek.

Amy, RN: Why are you screaming now?

Mrs. Zeller: Because it's coming out. [Screaming] It's coming out. Oh, Oh! Here it comes. Help me.

Amy, RN: [Firmly, but with a smile on her face, as if she is amused] Okay, okay. Now if you quiet down, I'll stay here with you but you have to quiet down. Some people may be sleeping. This *is* a hospital, you know [laughing]. I'll stay here with you until you're through.

THURSDAY

7:10

Liz, Sandy, Amy, and Sharon are sitting in the nurses' lounge waiting for Pat to enter and begin the morning report. Katie is off today. Sandy is looking at the unit census sheet.

Sandy, RN: I don't see Mr. Steele's name on here. Did he go?

Liz, RN: Yes, he did. Angie (the night nurse) told me that he slipped off quietly in his sleep between 2:00 and 2:30.

Sandy, RN: She said he was comfortable?

Liz, RN: Yes. He was asleep for the whole shift and never woke up.

Pat walks into the lounge and takes a seat at the table.

Sandy, RN: [To Pat] Did you know that Mr. Steele died?

Pat, RN: He slipped off at about 2:00 or 2:30 last night. Dr. Sims called back yesterday just after you left, at about 3:30 in the afternoon, and ordered the morphine drip. He was reluctant, but finally decided to go for it, that is, with a little urging. [She gives a knowing look.]

Sandy, RN: So he was on the morphine when he died?

Pat, RN: He sure was. I made sure to hang it as soon as Dr. Sims gave the go-ahead. It was up before 4:00 p.m. You were absolutely right, Sandy. As soon as the drip got going, Mr. Steele calmed down. Angie said that evenings told her that he didn't actually fall asleep until much later, but he was comfortable right away. That was what he really needed, the drip.

Sandy, RN: I'm sorry we didn't push for it earlier. He really didn't have to be that uncomfortable the past few days. I wish Dr. Sims wasn't so reluctant to use it. But at least Mr. Steele didn't suffer at the end. And, I guess, that's what counts. [She starts shuffling her papers, as if to signal that the conversation about Mr. Steele has ended.]

The report begins and Mr. Steele is not mentioned again. After a few moments, 48-year-old Mr. Heath is introduced on the tape. Pat stops the tape.

Pat, RN: He has an alcohol problem. He was transferred here to a private room from the other building. He's got a lot of money and he was telling me that he was in Southard [a private psychiatric institution with a fine reputation] and the place where Truman Capote was treated and knows a lot of those people.

Sharon, RN: When was he at Southard?

Pat, RN: I don't know. I have no idea. I don't get impressed with all that. I try to communicate to him that the only thing that matters is that today is a new day. And I really like him. He's a fag, but I can relate to fags and they don't frighten me, not like a female gay. He's also suspected of having AIDS.

Sandy, RN: Why?

Pat, RN: Because his bloodwork was off. But I don't think it's positive. Although he's not really on the ARU [Alcohol Recovery Unit] I'm going to expect him to do the ARU protocol.

Sharon, RN: What is that?

Pat, RN: He has to make his own bed, dispose of his own linen, and things like that.

Pat starts the tape recorder again.

7:20

Dr. Mitchell enters the nurses' lounge and interrupts the report. He has been making rounds, visiting each of his patients and has just come from the room of terminally ill Judy Palumbo, 37. Dr. Mitchell approaches Amy and begins speaking in an agitated tone.

Dr. Mitchell: I just came out of Judy's room and she's moaning. She's in incredible pain. [Angrily] Why is that happening? I ordered medication around the clock for her. I specifically said I didn't want to wait until she needed it, but that it should be given around the clock, regardless. Obviously, it wasn't given, and that's why she's like this. There's no reason for this.

Amy, RN: I haven't been in to see her yet and I didn't realize she was like that. But, you're right. There is absolutely no reason for it. I'll talk to nights to make sure this kind of thing never happens again. What do you want to do now?

Dr. Mitchell: Let's give her 10 [milligrams] of Valium IV.

Amy, RN: Sure. [She walks quickly to the medication room and prepares the medication.]

Dr. Mitchell and Amy walk together to the patient's room where Amy hands the medication syringe to Dr. Mitchell. The woman in the bed is thin and pale, her face distorted by pain. Her moans are soft as her head shakes form side to side, as if trying to deny what is happening.

Dr. Mitchell sits on the side of the bed and begins to administer the medication through her intravenous line. As he does so, Amy, sitting on the other side of the bed, holds both her patient's hands in her own as she attempts to reassure in a firm voice, "It will be okay, Judy. It will be okay in a minute." Amy releases Judy's hands only after she is deeply asleep.

7:40

Rejoining the group in the nurses' lounge, Amy is again speaking about Judy's pain. As she does so, her thumbs move agitatedly back and forth against the rings of the looseleaf binder she is holding.

Amy, RN: She's really bad. She's heavily medicated and sleeping soundly, but when she wakes she's in pain. She probably won't last too long. Her husband was in last night and was told she probably wouldn't make it through the night. They said he could take her wedding band if he wanted to but he couldn't bring himself to do it. He said he's wait until after. He won't be able to do it then either. So one of us will.

All are looking down at their assignment sheets. No one says anything for a moment or two. Then Pat starts the tape again.

9:30

Liz is caring for Mr. Kelly today because Katie is off. Mr. Kelly is barely conscious, opening his eyes from time to time only when he is moved. When his eyes open, they show no pain, only emptiness and waiting. His arms lie limp at his sides. His skin is as gray as his hair. His respirations are noisy from the fluids that have accumulated in his lungs. Every breath is an effort. When he is left alone he falls asleep, an escape from the waiting.

Liz provides minimal care for Mr. Kelly, just enough to make him comfortable without overtaxing him by moving him around more than necessary. She works slowly, being careful with his weakened painful limbs as she gently moves them. From time to time, she comments to Mr. Kelly: "There, now. I'll be done in a minute," or, "I know how difficult this is for you." Mr. Kelly does not answer. All his available energy is consumed by the act of breathing. When Liz is finished with Mr. Kelly, she busies herself around the room, putting things in their places. Mrs. Kelly arrives a few moments later.

Mrs. Kelly: How is he?

Liz, RN: No change.

Mrs. Kelly: No change?

Liz, RN: He's weak. Why don't you tell him you're here. He doesn't open his eyes too much, but he knows what's going on. Tell him you're here.

Mrs. Kelly: [Walks to bedside and picks up Mr. Kelly's hand in both of hers.] Honey?

Liz, RN: I'm leaving now, but if you need anything, just call. I'll be back in a little while.

Liz proceeds to Mrs. Tower's room. Seventy-nine-year-old Mrs. Tower has colon cancer; she is alert and oriented. Liz helps Mrs. Tower from the bed to a chair and brings her soap, washcloth, a towel, and a wash basin filled with warm water. Mrs. Tower begins washing herself while Liz makes the bed. The two chat while they busy themselves with their tasks, washing and bed making.

Liz, RN: Where do you live?

Mrs. Tower: In the ghetto.

Liz, RN: Ghetto?

Mrs. Tower goes on to explain that she lives in a retirement community and refers to this as "the ghetto." Liz finishes making the bed by this time and instructs Mrs. Tower to ring the call bell when she is finished washing so that Liz can assist her with a fresh gown. She leaves Mrs. Tower's room and proceeds to Mrs. Ray's. Mrs. Ray, 79, has had a stroke. She is confused, often combative, and awaiting nursing home placement. She has been nonverbal since her admission several weeks earlier.

Liz prepares fresh linens and a basin of water with which to wash Mrs. Ray, who, upon seeing Liz, snarls and spits. Liz approaches Mrs. Ray's bed.

Liz, RN: [Softly but firmly] Now, now, baby. Come on. I'm just going to wash you.

As Liz proceeds to wash Mrs. Ray in silence, Mrs. Ray tries to push Liz's hands away with her own.

Liz, RN: You act as if I'm being mean to you. I'm not being mean to you.

She then works quickly with no attempts at further communication. Mrs. Ray lies in silence, watching Liz's every move with a wary look on her face, saying nothing.

When Liz finishes with Mrs. Ray, she returns to the doorway of Mr. Kelly's room. Looking in, she sees Mr. Kelly lying quietly with his eyes closed. Mrs. Kelly is sitting in a chair next to the bed watching television.

Liz, RN: [To Mrs. Kelly from the doorway] Can I get you anything?

Mrs. Kelly: No thanks. I'm okay for now.

Liz, RN: Okay. But just holler if you need anything.

Liz walks to the nurses' lounge and pours herself a cup of coffee. She sits in a chair at the table and sips her coffee, staring at the wall. Liz has a medical check-up later in the afternoon, which she has semi-annually since her mastectomy a few years ago. Sandy walks into the lounge.

Sandy, RN: [In a concerned tone] How are you doing?

Liz, RN: [Very loud, in a voice that tries to convince] Oh, fine. Just fine. Why shouldn't I be doing fine?

Sandy, RN: Come on, Liz. It's me, Sandy. Remember?

Liz, RN: Does it show?

Sandy, RN: You mean that you're nervous about this afternoon? No, it doesn't show. But I know how you feel. And that's because I'd feel exactly the same way.

Liz, RN: I thought I'd be okay by now. You know, not anxious about it anymore. But there's always that chance that they'll find it [cancer] in another place.

Sandy, RN: Look, why don't you relax for awhile. You deserve it. I'll cover your patients for you. And Peggy can help me.

Liz, RN: That's silly. I'm really fine. And I'm much better off being busy, anyway.

Sandy, RN: Well, why don't you take some extra time for lunch? It's not that busy here today anyway. And it would be nice for you to go out for lunch. That'd be a nice change. And you could take a walk near the river. Just to get out for awhile.

Liz, RN: [Getting up from the chair and putting her arm around Sandy] Now, Sandy honey. I'm just fine. You worry too much. Do you know that?

Sandy, RN: [Annoyed] Liz, you're always taking care of everyone else but you never let anyone take care of you! Why can't you let us take care of you when you need it?

Liz, RN: But I don't need anyone to take care of me. I'm fine. Really.

Sandy, RN: Okay. Well, if you change your mind just let me know and I'll do some of your work. I really wish you'd let me do something.

Liz, RN: You can let me go back to work and get my work done. Come on! Sandy shrugs and both leave the lounge.

10:30

Pat is sitting at the table in the nurses' lounge with Mrs. Vega, who is sipping a cup of coffee provided by Pat. Mrs. Vega and her husband, who is 65 and terminally ill with cancer, have been married just eight months. They had been planning to retire within the next few months to travel when he was diagnosed with advanced metastatic cancer. Mr. Vega had major abdominal surgery a few days earlier and is recovering slowly. His disease has spread quickly and he is expected to live only a few more months. Mrs. Vega lost her first husband to leukemia.

Mrs. Vega: How is he?

Pat, RN: I'm not going to give you false hope. But he's doing very well with the surgery. I had to medicate him earlier but now he's comfortable.

They continue to speak about Mr. Vega's anticipated dietary needs, Mrs. Vega's need to hold off on her retirement plans, the type of chemotherapy Mr. Vega would receive, the extent of care he will require at home, and whether they could travel. Pat is holding Mrs. Vega's hand on the table top.

Pat, RN: [Gently] The things that seemed important to you before won't be important anymore. Different things will matter.

11:00

Pat walks to Mr. Heath's room and he greets her at the door. Looking into the room, she sees a perfectly made bed and a clean room.

Mr. Heath: I made my bed and threw my linen in the hamper [looking at Pat for approval].

Pat, RN: [No response.]

Mr. Heath: Is it okay to keep that out? [He points to a portable cassette player.]

Pat, RN: Did you ask your doctor?

Mr. Heath: I mean . . . is it safe?

Pat, RN: Oh. You don't have to worry about safety here. It'll be perfectly safe. This is not like the other place [referring to the Alcohol Recovery Unit in the main building].

Mr. Heath: Oh. What a relief. You should see that other place. It's terrible.

Pat, RN: I know what it's like. You're very lucky to have a private room.

Mr. Heath: I have to be at the ARU program in the main building at 11:30.

Pat, RN: I'll have to walk you over.

Several minutes later, Pat and Mr. Heath walk over to the main building. One the way Mr. Heath asks Pat if he is allowed to talk to her about his problems.

Pat, RN: You can say whatever you want. That's your problem.

Mr. Heath then proceeds to tell Pat about his alcohol problems, his ortho-pedic problems, and the insights he has gained into his life. Pat is silent. She drops him off at the ARU and proceeds back to Four South. Sandy has just brought a patient to X-ray and is also returning to Four South. Sandy and Pat meet in the elevator and Pat begins to tell Sandy of her conversation with Mr. Heath.

Pat, RN: I don't buy into all his stuff. He was just looking for approval in telling me that he made his bed but I didn't give any. He appeared to have much insight into his life but that was all a load of garbage. I know alcoholics very well because there are several in my family. In fact, I'm an alcoholic.

Sandy, RN: [In a matter-of-fact manner] Are you a recovered alcoholic or is this still a problem for you?

Pat, RN: No. I'm not recovered. And so I know the alcoholic personality. Alcoholics are always looking for approval from others—that's why they turn to drink. I use it to escape from things I don't want to do.

Sandy, RN: Does it interfere?

Pat, RN: Not with my work here. My work at home is a different story. If I have a few martinis after dinner, and alcoholics drink martinis, then I can sit down with my feet up and do the crossword puzzle and not do the laundry or any of the other things I don't want to do. It doesn't interfere with my life in that I don't get drunk.

The elevator doors open onto Four South and the conversation is over.

11:45

Sandy is in Ms. Martin's room helping her pack her things in preparation for going home.

Sandy, RN: Now, who's coming to take you home?

Ms. Martin: My next-door neighbor. She's been great through this whole thing. A real lifesaver!

Sandy, RN: And she can help you at home if you need it?

Ms. Martin: Oh, yes. Although she has her hands full with four kids. But she's there if I need her. At least I don't feel so alone knowing that she's next door.

Sandy, RN: And you have your prescriptions, and your next doctor appointment, and your exercises?

Ms. Martin: [Laughing] Yes, yes. I have everything. You're such a worry wart. I'll be fine. Really. The Reach for Recovery representative is visiting me tomorrow, thanks to you. I really think I'll be okay. I'm just very tired. But I know that will get better as time passes.

Sandy, RN: You've been doing your exercises?

Ms. Martin: Sure have. I'm really okay about following directions with everything. [Her face becoming serious] The only problem I seem to have is looking at the darn thing. It's as if looking at it makes it bigger than life. It's so threatening. That's the only thing that scares me. [Blinks a few times and sniffs.]

Sandy, RN: Scares you?

Ms. Martin: You know. I look at it and it's not the scar or the mutilation that bothers me. It's the wondering whether or not they got it all. But Liz says that's normal and she still worries sometimes, even after all these years. So I guess I'm normal.

Sandy, RN: [Embracing Ms. Martin] Yes, you're very normal.

Ms. Martin returns the embrace and the two women stand together silently for a moment.

Sandy, RN: Okay, okay. Let's get going. No more of this mush.

Sandy picks up Ms. Martin's suitcase and a bag filled with her personal belongings. Ms. Martin smiles as they walk toward the nurses' station together.

1:15

Mr. Glaser, 67 years old and terminally ill with metastatic cancer, was unresponsive when he expired at 12:55. Amy, who was his nurse, calls to inform Mr. Glaser's physician of his patient's death. The physician states that he would notify Mrs. Glaser. Mrs. Glaser, however, is already en route to the hospital to visit her husband and arrives on Four South 20 minutes later.

When Mrs. Glaser steps off the elevator, the staff at the nurses' station is shocked to see her. All assumed the physician notified her of her husband's death. When Mrs. Glaser sees the expressions on the faces of those around her, she immediately knows that her husband is gone. She shrieks, begins sobbing, and leans weakly against the nurses' station. Liz immediately runs to support Mrs. Glaser and provide a chair for her. Amy is with another patient in a room near the nurses' station and Barbara is working in her office. Hearing the sobbing, both interrupt what they are doing and appear at once at Mrs. Glaser's side.

Mrs. Glaser: Look at me, will you. I act as if I didn't know it was coming. I'm acting like a real baby. And I'm such a nuisance to all of you.

Amy, RN: That's okay. That's what we're here for. You have a right to cry.

Barbara, RN: Yes. It's good to cry. Just let it all out [cradling Mrs. Glaser in her arms].

When Mrs. Glaser's sobbing begins to subside, Barbara brings her to Mr. Glaser's room to spend a few last moments with her husband.

Barbara, RN: [At Mr. Glaser's bedside] If you think you'll be all right, I'll leave you alone for a few moments if you like. Otherwise, I'll be happy to stay here with you.

Mrs. Glaser: [Clutching a tissue and wiping her eyes] No, it's all right. I'll be okay alone.

Barbara, RN: If you're sure, now. I'll be just outside the door in case you need me.

Barbara leaves the room.

1:45

Sharon is in Mrs. Hunt's room. Mrs. Hunt, 53 years old and the mother of nine children, is terminally ill with metastatic cancer. She is alert, oriented, and attempts to remain very much in control of her situation. Mrs. Hunt's husband, father, and two brothers are physicians and she is very knowledgeable about all aspects of her care. Mrs. Hunt looks flushed and uncomfortable. She complains of nausea.

Mrs. Hunt: I don't want to take something unless I really need it.

Sharon, RN: Well, that's up to you. But if you're nauseous you're better off taking it than waiting.

Mrs. Hunt: I don't want to vomit. But I've been okay for the past few hours.

Sharon, RN: That's probably because you've been taking the medication.

Mrs. Hunt: I hate injections.

Sharon, RN: Well this is a suppository. I really suggest that you take it.

Mrs. Hunt: I suppose you're right. I really don't want to vomit. I have some pain, but I can deal with that. It's the vomiting I can't tolerate.

Sharon makes Mrs. Hunt comfortable in bed and leaves the room to obtain the medication. She returns a few moments later with Mrs. Hunt's medication.

At that point, two of Mrs. Hunt's sisters who are visiting with her leave the room in order to give her some privacy. When Sharon emerges from the room, one sister starts a conversation.

Sister: I know something about this because I do volunteer work in a hospice in Virginia. I think she should take pain medications around the clock. They say it's more effective when it's taken that way rather than only when it's needed.

Sharon, RN: Yes. That's usually how it's recommended.

Sister: Maybe someone can talk to her and explain.

Sharon, RN: She really has a mind of her own and she's reluctant to take it. I'll try to talk to her in a little while when she's feeling less nauseous. Maybe I can help her to realize that it would really be best to take it around the clock.

Mrs. Hunt's sisters return to the room and Sharon walks down the hall.

2:30

Dr. Mitchell is making rounds and is preparing to visit Mrs. Hunt, who is now in a wheelchair in the solarium with eight members of her family. Sharon wheels Mrs. Hunt back to her room where Dr. Mitchell is waiting.

Dr. Mitchell: How are you doing today?

Mrs. Hunt: Oh, okay now. I just had something for nausea a little while ago and it's really helped me. I can't stand the thought of vomiting again. I'm having some pain [she holds her abdomen] but it's not all that bad. I had some jello before. So far I've tolerated it. But it's really a problem for me because there's not too much I can tolerate. I feel like a pest complaining so much.

Sharon, RN: You're not complaining. I'll call the dietitian for a consult. The two of you can get together and I'm sure you will be able to come up with some things you are able to tolerate.

Mrs. Hunt: That would be good.

Dr. Mitchell: And what about the pain.

Sharon, RN: Your sisters are concerned that you're not as comfortable as you could be.

Mrs. Hunt: I really don't want to take injections.

Dr. Mitchell: [With an air of levity] Look. Take your dope, will you? We're going to talk about you anyway—we talk about all the patients, you know. You won't get addicted and you need to have some relief.

Mrs. Hunt: Well, I don't want to start with the heavy-duty stuff yet. Not until I really need it. I'd rather wait with the heavy-duty stuff until later on in my illness.

Sharon, RN: [Looking at Mrs. Hunt with a puzzled look] What do you mean by "heavy duty"?

Mrs. Hunt: Like morphine.

Sharon, RN: Let's see. Now you're talking Dilaudid.

Mrs. Hunt: That's right. I don't want to start on the morphine yet.

Sharon, RN: Morphine and Dilaudid are comparable. You're taking two milligrams of Dilaudid. That's the same as eight milligrams of morphine.

Mrs. Hunt: Oh! Then I'm already using that. [Seems relieved, rather than upset.]

Sharon, RN: Yes. And if you take it all around the clock you can actually take less of it for it to be effective in controlling your pain.

Mrs. Hunt: That means I won't build up a tolerance.

Sharon, RN: It will be much better for your pain control [evading Mrs. Hunt's statement about building up a tolerance].

Mrs. Hunt: I'll think about it.

Sharon, RN: Why don't you do that? It's your decision.

Mrs. Hunt: Can I wash my hair?

Dr. Mitchell: Sure.

Mrs. Hunt: I know you need an order for everything around here. Is the order written?

Dr. Mitchell: [Laughs] That makes us appear so powerful. Actually, it's the nurses who run everything around here. They let us write some orders to make us feel important, but it's they who are really running the show.

They all laugh and Sharon wheels Mrs. Hunt back to the solarium to join her family. Sharon then joins Dr. Mitchell at the nurses' station.

Sharon, RN: She has a mind of her own and needs time to make her own decisions. She's very knowledgeable about her situation and wants to retain complete control. I wish she'd accept some more pain medication though.

(Mrs. Hunt died two days later. She had become very nauseous and had a difficult time with pain control, refusing to take her medications. Finally, she consented to a morphine drip Friday evening and was comfortable at the end. Her family was with her.)

2:50

Sharon is preparing to leave the unit for the day and is making last rounds on all her patients. When she enters Mr. Sharpe's room, she finds him resting in bed watching television, his leg elevated on a pillow. Mr. Sharpe, 37, was in an automobile accident seven months ago, had surgery for an injury to his leg, and has a stubborn wound infection. He was admitted to Four South the previous day for intravenous antibiotic treatment. Earlier in the day Sharon changed his dressing, irrigated his wound, and provided his intravenous therapy.

Sharon, RN: Hi there! I'm leaving and wanted to stop in to say good-bye. How's the leg?

Mr. Sharpe: Not too bad. I had some pain medicine before and it's feeling pretty good now. I think this thing [pointing to the intravenous tubing in his arm] has a problem, though. It doesn't seem to be running right.

Sharon, RN: [Carefully examining the tubing and Mr. Sharpe's arm] Let's see. Does this hurt? [Sharon presses gently on Mr. Sharpe's arm.]

Mr. Sharpe: Ouch! You sure know how to hurt a guy, don't you?

Sharon, RN: This needs to be changed. That's why it's not running right. [Sharon shuts off the intravenous line.] I'll be right back with a new set and I'll change it for you.

Sharon disappears for a few minutes and returns with equipment to discontinue Mr. Sharpe's intravenous line and restart another in the other arm. While she works, she attempts to chat with Mr. Sharpe, asking him about the sensation and circulation in his toes, whether or not he keeps his leg elevated in his sleep, and how his family is managing while he is in the hospital. Mr. Sharpe responds, but only minimally, to most of Sharon's questions.

Sharon, RN: Well, what about your family? How are they managing?

Mr. Sharpe: Okay, I guess. What do you expect? I've been in bed for seven months, on and off, being cared for by nurses. And some of them are great, but some of them are really something. One showed up for work in black tight slacks and a black polo with writing on it.

Sharon, RN: Come on! And you didn't love it?

Mr. Sharpe: No! It's terrible when you have to depend on people and you don't even know if they know what they're doing. And my doctors haven't even been in yet to write orders for these wound irrigations. Here I am lying in the hospital and they haven't even been in!

Sharon, RN: Well, I did the irrigation just like they ordered. And the doctors ordered the antibiotics. That's what you're here for. And the wound looks good. I don't think there's any active infection on the outside. The antibiotics are for what's on the inside.

Mr. Sharpe: I know, but . . . oh well.

Sharon, RN: I know how discouraging it is for you to be in and out [of the hospital] for so long. And I don't blame you for being upset.

Mr. Sharpe: [Smiles] I guess I'm just being a nuisance. But, you're right. It's just that I'm upset. Thanks for understanding.

Sharon returns the smile, pats Mr. Sharpe's hand, and leaves with a wave of her hand.

Sharon, RN: See you tomorrow.

FRIDAY

7:15

Liz, Katie, and Amy are sitting at the table in the nurses' lounge ready to begin the report. Sharon is taking a moment to look in on her patients. Sandy and Pat are off today, and Liz is in charge of the unit.

Katie, RN: How'd you make out yesterday, Liz?

Liz, RN: You mean at the doctor's?

Katie, RN: What else do you think I mean?

Liz, RN: Just fine. I'm clean. Clean as a whistle. See, I told you gals there was nothing to worry about. You're all just a bunch of worry warts.

Katie, RN: Oh, like you never worry about it.

Liz, RN: [Smiles sheepishly.]

Katie, RN: Well, we're all relieved.

Liz, RN: *You're* relieved. How d'ya think I feel? I know I put up a big front. But I'm glad that's over for now.

Katie and Amy wait for Liz to start the taped report. Their pens are poised and ready.

Liz, RN: I need to change the assignments today. [To Katie] Honey, you'll have rooms 441–450.

Katie, RN: How many patients is that?

Liz, RN: Nine. Is that too much?

Amy, RN: [In defense of Katie] Yes, it sure is!

Liz, RN: [Erasing on her patient census sheet] Well, let me see how else I can do this. There's not really too much of a choice.

The final assignment results in an extremely heavy patient assignment for Amy, who does not have the help of a nurse's aide today. Her assignment includes four patients requiring total care ("completes") and one patient requiring much assistance.

Amy, RN: [Angrily, to Liz] That isn't even my area [of the unit]. I don't know the patients and can't possibly take care of all those completes.

Liz, RN: Well, I don't know what else to do. The floor's heavy.

Amy sits silently for the remainder of the report.

Liz, RN: Nights said that Mr. Kelly was fading.

Katie, RN: I'd be surprised if he makes it through the day. It'll be a blessing for them both [Mr. and Mrs. Kelly] if he goes.

Liz, RN: Well, just let me know if you need any help, honey.

Sharon, RN: [Entering the nurses' lounge] It seems like it's Black Friday around here today. Mrs. Fowler is on her way. She's totally unresponsive and her respirations are gurgling. I don't think she'll make it through the morning.

Katie, RN: Has anyone been in to visit her at all?

Sharon, RN: She has no family, just one friend. An elderly lady who lives next door. She was in yesterday afternoon and I told her that Mrs. Fowler was imminent.

Liz, RN: Will you call her?

Sharon, RN: I guess so.

Katie, RN: Gee. It's really awful that some people are all alone in life.

Sharon, RN: I'm not really sure which is worse. I mean being alone like Mrs. Fowler or leaving a young family like Judy Palumbo. She's not alone, but look at her family. There's a husband and two young kids. They're going through hell.

Katie, RN: And I can't believe she's still hanging on. I would have thought she'd have gone long before this. I wonder why some people have to suffer so long.

Sharon, RN: And it's not just her that's suffering. It's Ken and those kids.

Liz, RN: Listen, ladies. If we don't get started, we'll never make it through the day. Let's go.

7:50

Following completion of the report, Liz remains in the lounge for a few moments while Katie, Amy, and Sharon leave and approach the nurses's station. Amy is still seething about her assignment.

Amy, RN: [To Sharon] Boy! Did I get screwed today.

Amy replaces her patient medication cardex while Sharon sits down at the counter and phones Mrs. Fowler's friend.

Sharon, RN: [Gently] This is the nurse at the hospital. I wanted to let you know that Mrs. Fowler is pretty bad.

Meanwhile, Amy proceeds to one of her patient's rooms. She enters the room of a 75-year-old acutely ill woman.

Amy, RN: Come on, sweetie. I'm going to help you with breakfast [as she raises the back of the bed and sets up the breakfast tray]. Can you see [as she rummages though the drawer in the nightstand for the patient's eyeglasses]?

Patient: No. I don't need them.

Amy, RN: Okay. Do you have your dentures?

Patient: Yes [showing them with a smile].

Amy, RN: Good. After you eat, I'll come back and wash you.

Amy waits at the bedside to see that her patient is able to manage her breakfast. Seeing this, Amy leaves the room.

8:35

Sharon is giving Mrs. Fowler her morning care. Mrs. Fowler is unresponsive throughout, moaning occasionally. No verbal interaction between Sharon and Mrs. Fowler occurs during the 25-minute procedure.

8:50

Mrs. Fowler's friend arrives and stops at the nurses' station. Helen summons Sharon.

Sharon, RN: She's pretty bad.

Friend: May I go in and see her?

Sharon, RN: Sure. I'll go with you.

Both women disappear down the hallway toward Mrs. Fowler's room. Mrs. Fowler's friend visits briefly, but Mrs. Fowler is unresponsive, seemingly oblivious to her presence.

Sharon, RN: There really isn't anything you can do.

Friend: I guess you're right. Please call me when . . . it happens?

Sharon, RN: Of course.

With Sharon's help, Mrs. Fowler's friend gathers all Mrs. Fowler's personal belongings and leaves the unit.

Sharon stops in to Mrs. Fowler's room every 30 minutes or so throughout the morning to see if she is still breathing. She discovers, during her third such visit to Mrs. Fowler's room, that Mrs. Fowler has, indeed, stopped breathing. Mrs. Fowler died alone. Sharon calmly walks to the nurses' station.

Sharon, RN: [To Liz and Helen] Mrs. Fowler's gone. Call the house doctor to pronounce her and I'll call her friend. [Mutters, as if to herself] One down and one to go [referring to Mr. Kelly].

9:30

Katie is preparing to bathe Mr. Kelly. She washes only his hands and face since, she explains later, he is imminently terminal; giving him a complete bath is "unnecessary and would only add to his stress." Her care is slow, methodical, and gentle. There is no eye contact with Mr. Kelly. Katie makes him as comfortable as possible, positioning him in a sitting position to facilitate his breathing. The only verbalization with Mr. Kelly occurs toward the end of his care:

Katie, RN: There. Is that more comfortable? . . . Isn't that better? [She kisses his forehead gently.]

Mr. Kelly does not respond. His respirations are increasingly noisy and his face is dusky. Katie tidies the room and leaves.

10:40

Amy and Sharon are standing outside Mrs. Ray's room.

Amy, RN: My whole assignment is like this [motioning toward Mrs. Ray] today. It's just not fair.

Sharon, RN: Mrs. Fowler just went. At least it's over for her.

Amy, RN: Oh. Was anyone with her?

Sharon, RN: No. But she didn't know the difference. She's been out of it for a couple of days.

Amy, RN: Poor thing.

Sharon, RN: I've got to keep going. Call me if you need help with Mrs. Ray.

Amy, RN: Okay. But you have your hands full, too.

Amy enters Mrs. Ray's room and begins her morning care, bathing her as Mrs. Ray grunts angrily.

Amy, RN: [Looking Mrs. Ray straight in the eye from a distance of approximately 12 inches] Now let me wash you so you'll be all nice and clean.

Mrs. Ray: [Fights and spits.]

Amy, RN: [Firmly, again with direct eye contact] Now stop that! Do you want me to tape your mouth?

Mrs. Ray stops spitting at Amy and allows her to bathe and powder her front. Amy works quickly, gently, and silently.

Amy, RN: Now I'm going to turn you over so we can wash your back. If you understand what I'm saying, make a sound.

Mrs. Ray: [No response.]

Amy again attempts to explain to Mrs. Ray what she is about to do. When Mrs. Ray offers no response, Amy, assisted by Sharon, turns her and completes her care by washing and massaging her back.

Amy, RN: [To Sharon] I hated to call you in here to help. I know how swamped you are today.

Sharon, RN: Don't be silly. You could never do this alone.

Amy, RN: I'd have called Liz. She certainly has more time than you. Fat chance of getting help from her, though.

Sharon, RN: [No reply.]

Amy and Sharon position Mrs. Ray on her side. Sharon places a pillow under Mrs. Ray's head and leaves the room. Amy, alone at the bedside, repositions the pillow to make Mrs. Ray more comfortable.

11:00

Sharon is in a room shared by two women. One is 69 years old and suffering from cholangitis (inflammation of the bile ducts). The other, 58, recently had a cholecystectomy (surgical removal of the gallbladder). Both are alert, oriented, and ambulatory. Sharon is changing an intravenous medication bottle and tubing. While doing this, she chats amicably with both. One mentions that she finally had baked ham and sauerkraut, for which she had been longing for quite some time but was unable to tolerate because it made her ill. Sharon, assesses various aspects of both ladies' illnesses while chatting with them in what appears to be a casual manner.

When Sharon is finished with her work in that room, she proceeds to the next room, shared by two men. One is 25 years old and has chronic hepatitis. He is extremely interested in his treatment regimen, asking frequent questions of his nurses. He is about to undergo a liver biopsy. His roommate, 50 years old, was admitted for diagnostic testing related to a problem with his esophagus. He has just returned to his room from an esophageal endoscopy.

Sharon assists this patient from the stretcher to his bed.

Sharon, RN: I have to take your vital signs. And no smoking yet. You're still too woozy [from the sedative he received before the endoscopy].

Sharon takes his blood pressure, pulse, and respirations, then prepares to assist the other patient's physician with the liver biopsy. She is at the bedside for approximately ten minutes in silence. Upon completion of the test, she instructs the patient to remain in bed, "just like we discussed before," and leaves the room with the test equipment.

12:45

Katie is with Mr. Kelly. He is imminently terminal. He is now semiconscious, opening his eyes less and less frequently. His circulation is beginning to fail as evidenced by a blue mottling of his legs. His respirations are more labored and noisy and he is quite restless, although he is receiving morphine via a continuous intravenous drip.

Katie medicates him with Thorazine to relieve his restlessness. She does not suction his respiratory passages because the fluids have accumulated so deep in his lungs that suctioning would succeed only in alarming Mr. Kelly and further decreasing his blood oxygen levels. Katie is just leaving Mr. Kelly's room when Mrs. Kelly arrives. She walks into her husband's room, looks at him helplessly, walks back into the hallway, and turns to Katie, who follows her.

Mrs. Kelly: Should I go home and come back later when he's feeling better?

Katie, RN: [Gently] You can do what you like. He'll be quieter in a few minutes because I just medicated him, but he won't be much different later. There's really not much more we can do for him [with much eye contact while gently touching Mrs. Kelly's arm]. Why don't you go in for a few minutes and tell him you're here.

Mrs. Kelly returns to the room and spends about five minutes with her husband. Mr. Kelly opens his eyes occasionally but is unable to respond to his wife. Mrs. Kelly then returns to the hallway where Katie is waiting.

Mrs. Kelly: I'm going home to get my sister-in-law. She's there by herself and I'll bring her back with me.

Katie, RN: That's a good idea.

Mrs. Kelly leaves the unit.

1:30

Mrs. Kelly returns and knocks hesitantly at the half-closed door of her husband's room. Katie emerges from the room and joins Mrs. Kelly in the hallway with her sister-in-law. Katie requests that they walk to the solarium together.

Mrs. Kelly: [Standing in the solarium and pointing to her sister-in-law] I brought my moral support.

Katie, RN: That's okay. You need it. [Gently, with an understanding look, she sits with Mrs. Kelly and her sister-in-law.] This is very difficult for you.

Mrs. Kelly: How long?

Katie, RN: I don't think it'll be too much longer. But it's hard to say for sure. It could be an hour or it could be tomorrow. It's impossible to say exactly [with direct eye contact].

Mrs. Kelly: I understand. If only he were more comfortable. His breathing is so terrible.

Katie, RN: With the morphine drip he's really comfortable. Right now it's harder for you than for him.

Mrs. Kelly: He didn't even know I was there before.

Katie, RN: I saw a response in his eyes when you walked into the room.

Mrs. Kelly: Really? Maybe I should go back in there, then.

1:55

Katie, Mrs. Kelly, and her sister-in-law return to Mr. Kelly's room. Mr. Kelly, now completely unresponsive, appears peaceful. His respirations are quieter. Katie encourages Mrs. Kelly to sit in a chair next to the bedside. There she holds Mr. Kelly's hand in both of hers. Her sister-in-law stands behind her, leaning on Mrs. Kelly's chair, with one hand on Mrs. Kelly's shoulder, the other clutching a tissue. Katie moves to the opposite side of the bed and takes Mr. Kelly's free hand in one of hers. Her other hand is supporting a towel under Mr. Kelly's nose and mouth to catch draining secretions. (Katie later reports, "I didn't want her to have to see the secretions.") From time to time, Katie unobtrusively places her fingers on Mr. Kelly's carotid pulse. She is monitoring him closely, but not noticeably.

2:00
Father James, summoned earlier by Katie, arrives and is at the foot of the bed. Katie, Mrs. Kelly, and her sister-in-law are praying with Father James. All are weeping. At the conclusion of the prayers, Mrs. Kelly looks questioningly at Katie, who responds to Mrs. Kelly's nonverbal question.
Katie, RN: It'll only be a few minutes.
Mrs. Kelly wipes her eyes as she looks lovingly at her husband.

2:14
Mr. Kelly expires peacefully. Katie gently lowers the back of the bed and tells Mrs. Kelly that she may be alone with her husband for a few minutes if she wishes.
Katie and the others wait for Mrs. Kelly outside the door, allowing her some last minutes of privacy with her husband. While waiting, Katie asks Helen to call Dr. Mitchell to advise him that his patient has expired and to call the house doctor to the unit to pronounce Mr. Kelly dead.

2:20
Mrs. Kelly tearfully emerges from the room.
Katie, RN: The house doctor is coming to pronounce him. I've called Dr. Mitchell to tell him. Why don't we go down the hall. There's a comfortable room there for you to sit for awhile.
Mrs. Kelly: Oh, Katie! I'm so glad you're here today.

2:50
Dr. Mitchell arrives on the unit and is directed to the room where Katie, Mrs. Kelly, and her sister-in-law are gathered.
Dr. Mitchell: I'm sorry.
Mrs. Kelly: I'm glad it was fast. God was merciful.
Dr. Mitchell: Yes. There was nothing more we could do. He was free of pain. At least we know that. If there's any way we can help . . .
Katie's hand is covering Mrs. Kelly's on the top of the table where it is resting. With her other hand, Katie wipes a tear from her cheek.

Several weeks following Mr. Kelly's death, Katie received the following note from Mrs. Kelly:

Dear Katie,

There really isn't any way I can tell you how much it meant to me to have you with me when Tom passed away. Your kindness and understanding were such a great comfort. Thank you very much for being there.

When Katie received the note, she commented, "Things like this make it all worthwhile."

Chapter 4

Beliefs and Behaviors of Four South Nurses

All the nurses studied had certain beliefs about the ways in which they cared for their patients and about the ways in which they lived their lives. Just as personal beliefs affect the behavior of all individuals, the nurses' beliefs had a profound influence on their nursing behavior. The nurses shared their beliefs about nursing and about life and death in semistructured personal interviews and impromptu conversations. This chapter explores the beliefs and behaviors of the nurses of Four South. When presenting data I obtained from interviews and conversations with the nurses, I shall refer to myself as "Nelda."

BELIEFS ABOUT NURSING

Philosophies of Nursing

Nurses spoke about their philosophies of nursing. Only two nurses incorporated specific nursing activities into their verbalized philosophies. Liz expressed the desire to "do more treatments," and Amy included the goal of "getting the patient better and out of the hospital."

When asked about their philosophies of nursing, two others spoke of fulfilling personal needs in themselves by helping others. One stated "Nursing makes me feel needed. People come to me with their problems. I help them and it makes me feel good."

One morning Katie approached the nurses' station waving a piece of paper with great pride. It was the letter of thanks that Mr. Kelly's wife had written to her. Katie said, "This makes me feel like I really *am* doing something worthwhile."

In helping Mr. Kelly to die and helping Mrs. Kelly to cope with his dying, Katie met a deep need within herself to do "something worthwhile."

Most people, when learning that a nurse works with the dying, assume that it is a depressing, emotionally draining, and most unpleasant task. It is interesting to note that the task of working with the dying may fulfill a particular need in the provider of care and, therefore, may be an experience of personal growth.

Sandy was reluctant to commit herself to a specific philosophy of nursing. Further discussion revealed that she believed a philosophy of nursing changed "day by day" according to the needs of the patient and the abilities of the nurse.

> Some days I think it's about teaching, and some days it's just doing tasks like bathing because there's no time [to do] anything else. But, all in all, whatever it is that nursing is about, it involves helping people to live and to die in whatever way we are able to.

Philosophies of nursing were related to hospice nursing in various ways. Amy stated that comfort was the "main consideration" in hospice nursing: to keep the patient free from pain as well as to "ease the family's pain." She believes in "making the patient and family as comfortable as possible with dying, physically and emotionally." Often, this required that nurses assume the role of patient advocate, interceding or arguing in the patient's behalf when necessary.

One morning as Sandy and Amy were writing their nurses' notes in the lounge, Linda Remm, the hospice coordinator, entered and announced that, at the physician's orders, she had just discontinued the intravenous morphine drip and hung a bottle of dextrose for Mr. Taylor. Mr. Taylor, Amy's patient, was 76 years old, semiconscious, and imminently terminal with lung cancer. In the past few days he had become increasingly restless and apprehensive; his pain was unrelieved by injections. He was comfortable only with the morphine drip, which had been in place for the past 24 hours. Both Amy and Sandy disagreed with the physician's decision to discontinue the medication and were visibly upset. Before Linda left the lounge, however, she assured them that she would obtain an order from the physician to restart the morphine for Mr. Taylor.

When Linda left, Amy and Sandy discussed ways in which a nurse may manipulate a physician into ordering a medication for a patient when it would be to the patient's benefit. The decision to order a medication rests entirely with the attending physician. When the nurses believe the physician's decisions may not be in the patient's best interest, usually when a physician is less experienced than the nurse, they often suggest to the physician that other medications or treatments be ordered. They talked about the guilt associated with such manipulation and agreed that this was somewhat mitigated by the necessity for nurses to assume the role of patient advocate, as Linda was doing for Mr. Taylor. The nurses recognized that Mr. Taylor could obtain a measure of comfort only with the morphine. His comfort was their goal and they would do whatever necessary to help him to be comfortable.

Being a patient advocate often involves risk-taking. According to Sandy, risk-taking is something for which a "good nurse" needs to be prepared. Her own willingness to take professional risks for the benefit of her patients was consistently demonstrated.

Sandy expressed concern that Ms. Martin, the 42-year-old woman with the new mastectomy, may not have been ready to go home because she lived alone and had no support system. Ms. Martin had not accepted her mastectomy and was teary when discussing it. In addition, a heavy menses was causing anemia and weakness. Sandy was upset that Dr. Norman had misinformed her patient about the procedure required to obtain a home health aide to assist her. Sandy repeatedly attempted to be tactful with Dr. Norman, explaining the situation and requesting him to order a visiting nurse evaluation for Ms. Martin. She continued to "suggest" that Dr. Norman order home assistance for Ms. Martin, even though he was becoming increasingly angry with Sandy. Sandy was willing to take a risk to obtain the best possible care for her patient.

In a private hospital such as MMC, attending physicians have final power and authority regarding their patients' care. This is often used to influence the ways in which nurses interact with physicians and the ways in which they care for their patients. Sandy has disagreed with physicians in the past regarding care for her patients and, when she believed it to be in her patients' best interests, has argued in their behalf. This has resulted in her being "written up" several times. Such complaints are placed in a nurse's personnel file and are reviewed when the nurse is eligible for a salary increase or promotion.

Holistic Care

Most nurses on Four South verbalized a holistic philosophy of nursing, a philosophy of caring for the "whole being." They spoke of meeting all of the patient's needs: physiological, emotional, and spiritual, i.e., the interrelatedness of body, mind, and spirit. Their highest priority was patient comfort and, when comfort was achieved, the emotional component of care. Patient comfort was a continual concern of the nurses on Four South. When patients suffered, it touched the nurses deeply and they reacted at times with anger and at times with tears. Sandy and Amy showed their anger with Dr. Sims when he discontinued Mr. Taylor's intravenous morphine drip. Katie's tears flowed when she recalled 37-year-old Judy Palumbo's pain. Their caring about their patients' comfort was obvious.

Prioritizing their patients' needs, the nurses recognized that physical comfort must be assured before emotional needs could be addressed. They recognized that when an individual is experiencing pain the physiological sensation of the pain often overtakes consciousness so that nothing else matters. Getting rid of the pain, then, is the first order of business. Once the pain has been relieved and comfort achieved, emotional needs begin to surface and can be attended to. This is consistent with Maslow's (1970) hierarchy of human needs.

Sharon summarized the goal of nursing as "making people as healthy, knowledgeable, and comfortable as one possibly can." Emphasis was placed on educating patients toward this goal. Katie spoke of giving patients the "benefit of your knowledge to improve the quality of their lives." Four South nurses consistently taught their patients about their medical conditions. For example, Sandy taught Mr. Young about his medications and their side effects. But Four South nurses did not limit their teaching to facts. For example, Katie taught Mr. Brent how to communicate with his wife, how to tell her that he loved her:

Mr. Brent: She knows how much I love her.

Katie, RN: [Gently] Yes, I'm sure she does. But I believe you will both feel a lot better if you talk about those things. It's really important, you know.

Spiritual Care

Most nurses were able to easily articulate the implementation of a philosophy of nursing that included both physiological and emotional care. Spiritual care, however, was more difficult for them to define and, when defined, was initially associated with religion.

Sandy, Amy, and Katie were in the nurses' lounge discussing a forthcoming continuing professional education seminar that emphasized a holistic approach to nursing care. One of the objectives of the seminar referred to a spiritual component of care.

Nelda: How are spiritual needs assessed and, if a patient has unmet spiritual needs, how are they met? I imagine that's a tricky thing to do.

Sandy, RN: Well, if the patient is close to death, we'll call the priest or the chaplain.

A discussion ensued about meeting patients' spiritual needs. Sandy, Amy, and Katie all agreed that there was always a member of the clergy available within the hospital for those who were near death.

Katie, RN: Well, I'll always call the priest if that's what they want. At the end, those with a faith—it really doesn't matter in what, but a faith in something—find it easier. Not always, but as a rule. I've seen people with faith panic and I've seen those without faith accept it. But, as a rule, it's much easier with faith.

Nelda: So spiritual needs are associated with a religion?

Katie, RN: Not necessarily with a particular religion. For example, a priest can see someone who is not Catholic. Or a rabbi can see a Christian. They have an ability to help even if they are not of the same faith.

From these comments, it appeared that spiritual care was perceived as religious in nature and always delegated to a clergyman. In a subsequent discussion, however, Barbara explained how nurses provided spiritual care through the use of appropriate resources:

Barbara, RN: It's not true that the nurses don't get involved in spiritual care. But we don't have the "power," and I think that's what they want. That makes them feel closer to God. But I pray with them. And I say a prayer myself for them. And I listen to them. And if we're busy and can't stay with them we make sure someone stays with them. But there are people who are better at it than I am and I always use my resources. They should have the best available.

Initially, it appeared that meeting patients' spiritual needs was not perceived by the nurses to be a nursing function. Barbara clarified this, however, by explaining that Four South nurses did, in fact, meet their patients' spiritual needs in two ways. When nurses perceived patients' spiritual needs as religious, they appropriately utilized available resources to meet those needs. That is, they initiated spiritual care by "experts" in the field who were better prepared to meet patients' needs, often through religious rites and sacraments. Believing that clergy were better prepared to meet their patients' religious needs, the nurses indirectly provided this care by summoning a chaplain, priest, or rabbi.

There was another way, however, that nurses attended to patients' spiritual needs. There is an aspect of spiritual care associated with a nurturing of the spirit in a humanistic, rather than religious, sense. This nurturing is done through the sharing of one's presence and through compassion. Four South nurses nurtured their patients' spirits by being with them, listening to them, and caring about them.

Sandy provided spiritual care, in a nurturing sense, to terminally ill Mrs. Salmon. Mrs. Salmon had been admitted the previous evening. She had advanced cancer and knew she was dying. When Sandy entered Mrs. Salmon's room on her initial morning nursing rounds, she found Mrs. Salmon in bed "looking very much alone." Assessing Mrs. Salmon's needs, Sandy requested Amy to "look in" on her other patients so that Sandy would be free to remain with Mrs. Salmon for a while.

Returning to Mrs. Salmon's room, Sandy sat down on the edge of the bed. Taking one of Mrs. Salmon's trembling hands and holding it firmly in both her own, she looked seriously at Mrs. Salmon.

Sandy, RN: It's not easy is it?

Mrs. Salmon: [Looking down to avoid eye contact with Sandy] No.

Sandy, RN: How can I help?

Mrs. Salmon: [Now looking directly at Sandy] Oh, Sandy! Just your being here is a help.

Sandy, RN: Well, I'm here.

The two sat together in silence for many minutes.

Nurses Are Human

It is natural for individuals to prefer some people to others and to avoid those people who are not preferred. Nurses are no different. Four South nurses readily admitted biases toward some types of patients and against others. Categories described tended to be dualistic: terminal and nonterminal, hospice and nonhospice, men and women, old and young, surgical and medical, cancer and noncancer, pampered and unspoiled.

Nurses made statements such as:

I hate to take care of abdominal hysterectomies and gallbladders. They're potsy [slow] and whining and tend to be pampered people.

I am more sympathetic toward cancer patients.

Lumbosacral spine patients are whining and manipulative; I hate 'em.

These nurses readily acknowledged their human biases but also maintained that the needs of all their patients were similar and that they "acted the same to all of them," regardless of how they felt. According to Sandy, "The basic needs are the same for all—comfort, hands-on care, and emotional support." Her message was that patients against whom a nurse may be biased have the same needs as those patients who are "more likable." The personal biases were overcome to allow the Four South nurses to provide comprehensive and holistic nursing care to all their patients.

An example of observed nursing care unaffected by a personal bias was Liz's care for Ms. Myers, her 28-year-old, unmarried, black, pregnant patient who was scheduled for an abortion. During the morning report one day, Liz commented to Sandy:

She's pregnant—five months—and going to the city for a therapeutic abortion. She had an abortion a couple of years ago. She's not married and has a history of lupus . . . I can't feel sorry for her. She knows what she's doing. And, of course, she's black. Who else would be in that situation?

Liz was admittedly prejudiced against unmarried women becoming pregnant and believed that this was a problem encountered much more frequently in the black population: another prejudice. Later in the morning, however, Liz was observed in Ms. Myers's room feigning empathy when she believed her patient needed it.

Ms. Myers: It's so hard to know if I'm doing the right thing. But I just can't go through and have the baby. I do want the abortion. I mean, I've given it a lot of thought and it's the best thing for me to do. But, even so, I feel awful about it [crying].

Liz, RN: [Pauses momentarily, then walks across the room to Ms. Myers and takes her hand.] Sure you do, honey. This is not an easy thing to do. I know just what you're going through. But, no matter how much you know it's the right thing, it's still hard. I don't blame you for crying.

Liz did not let her personal biases affect her ability to reach out to her patient. She acted the same as if she were not racially and morally prejudiced.

Interpersonal dynamics such as disagreements among staff or problems of a personal nature did not affect the ways in which nurses interacted with their patients. For example, when Liz, who was in charge on Four South, changed Amy's patient assignment, Amy became angry. However, her anger did not interfere with her patient care. Immediately following her expression of anger to Sharon, Amy proceeded to one of her patients, a 75-year-old acutely ill woman. Amy took the time to be sure that her elderly patient was comfortably eating. She demonstrated patience, caring, and understanding of her patient's needs, showing no evidence whatsoever of her personal anger with her assignment or with Liz.

Amy, RN: Come on, sweetie. I'm going to help you with breakfast [as she raised the back of the bed and set up the breakfast tray]. Can you see [as she rummaged through the drawer in the nightstand for the patient's eyeglasses]?

Amy, like Liz, admitted to certain biases. Nevertheless, she was observed consistently interacting with her patients in a most caring and attentive manner. I questioned her about this:

Nelda: I noticed that when you're with a patient, regardless of their condition or mental status, you have the most beautiful smile on your face and you seem to be doting on every word they say with genuine interest.

Amy, RN: [Laughs.]

Nelda: I wondered because you always seem so very interested in all they say, even when Mrs. Pizzo was describing her bowel movement in great detail yesterday.

Amy, RN: [Laughing] As long as they believe it.

Nelda: What do you mean?

Amy, RN: It's a put on!

Nelda: A put on?

Amy, RN: If I can't be ecstatically happy in doing this particular task, or if I have a particular problem at this time, I won't take it out on you as a patient. You, as a patient, have a right to the best possible care, delivered with a smile. And that's what you'll get.

And the Show Must Go On

Amy articulated a view apparently shared by the Four South nurses. They believed that quality nursing care included an attitude of acceptance of and interest in the patient. It is reasonable to assume that a nurse may, for a variety of personal reasons, be unable or unwilling to *feel* accepting of or interested in a particular patient at a given time. If the nurse can, however, believably feign acceptance and interest, the patient will receive the benefit of quality holistic nursing care.

Providing quality nursing care was the highest priority of the Four South staff. Nothing was permitted to affect that care, certainly not the moods or the feelings of the participant nurses, who demonstrated their conviction that nursing is a show that "must go on" regardless of the nurses' personal needs at the time of their "performance." The audience (patients) are entitled to the best possible performance and the actors (nurses) provided this to the best of their ability. That ability is dependent, however, on time constraints, as we shall see in the discussion of "busyness" in Chapter 5.

Nursing the Dying

Katie believes that the dying patient is no different from the acutely ill patient in that "people are alive when they're dying and want to laugh and enjoy basic things, even though they're dying." This means that, while death need not be denied, a nurse's preoccupation with a patient's impending death is not therapeutic for the patient. Terminally ill patients need to enjoy things like food, company, and entertainment. They need to be free, at times, from thoughts of their impending death. Pat believes that "hospice is really critical care—critical in that we deal with death." Her message is that death is a critical issue in the lives of all of us.

Nursing the dying means facing death on a day-to-day basis in a society where death is shunned. According to Toynbee and Koestler (1976), we live in a culture that considers death "un-American." The acute care subculture in which the Four South nurses function is designed to fight death. Death is considered a defeat. And yet, the nurses on Four South continually face it.

Amy admitted it was difficult, at times, to do "this kind" of work, stating, "Sometimes we laugh a lot. But it relieves the tension. And sometimes I think I just don't feel anything anymore. But then I find myself crying for no apparent reason."

The patient who precipitated these comments was 37-year-old Judy Palumbo, terminally ill with cancer and in great pain when awake. Amy recalled a moment at which the woman's pain was "out of control." She was screaming and clawing at Amy, who described this as "a horrible experience." Amy related how she held both her patient's hands in her own and tried to be reassuring while the physician administered an intravenous sedative. As Amy was speaking of this "horrible experience," a tear rolled down her cheek. It was, indeed, difficult for Amy to think about this dying woman's pain.

All spoke of helping terminally ill patients "get in touch with" and verbalize their feelings. According to Pat, "Many patients have to be taught how to die." This teaching involves helping patients acknowledge and express their emotions. At times, the teaching is planned, as in the following example of a nurse's comment about a terminally ill patient: "I've been watching her. She's probably ready to talk about [her diagnosis of cancer] now." The nurse assessed a terminally ill patient's readiness to speak about her diagnosis and planned to initiate a conversation that would help the patient face her condition.

At other times, the teaching was unplanned or spontaneous. For example, Katie did not plan to help Mr. Brent learn to communicate his feelings when she encouraged him to express his love and his fears to his wife.

Barbara believes one of the most important and difficult aspects of hospice nursing is not losing sight of the fact that family members are an integral part of the "patient unit" and must have their needs met. She states: "While this is difficult with all that has to be done for other patients, we must drop all else and be available."

When 67-year-old Mr. Glaser expired, Amy, who had been his nurse, called the physician and informed him of the man's death. The physician was unable to notify Mrs. Glaser, who was en route to the hospital to visit her husband. Unaware of her husband's death, Mrs. Glaser was unprepared when she arrived on Four South and reacted emotionally to the shock of learning about his death. Liz, Amy, and Barbara made themselves immediately available to Mrs. Glaser when she needed them. They provided physiological and emotional support for a grieving wife by being with her, providing a shoulder to cry on, normalizing her reaction by stating, "You have a right to cry," and by assisting her to say her final good-bye to her husband.

Yes, it *is* difficult to do "this kind" of work.

BELIEFS ABOUT LIFE AND DEATH

The Four South nurses, like all of us, must face the idea of their own deaths. It is, of course, impossible to separate the concept of death from the concept of life. And so, the nurses shared their beliefs about life and death.

Just as all participant nurses had given thought to their philosophies of nursing, all had given thought to the issues of life and death in their own personal philosophies. According to Katie, "Of course we think more about death than most people. We have to."

A "Good Death"

Death was viewed somewhat differently by each of the nurses, but was universally viewed as nonthreatening. Sharon maintained that death was inevitable and that she was not afraid of it. She had given much thought, however, to the way in which she might die. "I don't want to fall from a plane, for example." She also spoke of the need to raise her daughter and of not dying before her child was grown.

Amy's only fear was of the unknown: "I'd like to think that there's something after, but I don't know." Sandy verbalized ambivalence about death, speaking about a "life beyond, spirit and soul, and psychic happenings" that alluded to the concept of life after death.

Some of the nurses incorporated the idea of God and heaven in their philosophies of life and death. Liz shared that she was once frightened by death and then "decided to face it. That has helped. God is really with you. [Dying people] are not alone."

Pat believes that "We are born to die and be with God. Anger and sadness are there, but it is okay. I'm more interested living. I don't mind dying. I just don't want to do it!"

Barbara believes in living life to the fullest with short-term goals and sees death as an end to life but not an end to all being, believing as she does in heaven.

Katie summarized the feelings of many of the nurses regarding death: "It is natural; not mysterious or frightening. But it's a lonely thing to die."

Loneliness was a recurring theme that several nurses associated with death. As one explained: "No matter how many [people] are around [when you're dying], you still do it alone. No one goes with you. It's a solo act."

Some spoke of a loss of power that comes with thoughts of being terminally ill and of feelings of sadness about leaving loved ones behind. Barbara spoke of a "sadness at leaving but a rejoicing" about going to a peaceful existence with others who had died.

The nurses on Four South seemed to have reconciled thoughts and feelings of life and death within themselves before dealing with these issues in the care of their patients. Each had a definition of a "good death" for a patient:

The patient is comfortable, no severe pain. And the family lets go.

They go in their sleep or peacefully. It's kind of hard if you're alert.

Just to go to sleep if your feelings are not resolved.

Peaceful in mind and in comfort.

The family is present. Everything in order in their "house." Comfort. Peace with God.

They've accepted the fact [that they're dying] and their personal life is in order, like having made funeral arrangements. And no pain.

Pain free. Just stop breathing, no gurgling.

Some patients just can't face it. I think if they can't, they shouldn't have to.

Reaching emotional peacefulness.

A good death is whatever the particular patient wants and needs. For instance, if a patient has to resolve certain issues with a family member and does so, that is a good death for that patient. Or if they want to be asleep and are, that is a good death. But to be asleep is not for everyone. . . . A good death is, in essence, defined by each patient.

Accompanying the Dying

Feelings about being with a dying person at or near the time of death varied. The nurses expressed ambivalent feelings that included hurt, sorrow, relief, anxiety, depression, elation, traumatization, holiness, and "frozenness." Most agreed that the feelings experienced by the nurse depended upon the condition of the particular patient and on the acceptance of the death by the patient's family. According to Sharon, being with a person at the time of death is "different every time. Sometimes I feel relief. Sometimes I feel sorrowful. One 90-year-old said 'Goodbye' and died 15 minutes later. I felt teary but good. It was almost as if he were seeing the other side. He said, 'It's so beautiful.'"

Sandy described her feelings as anxious, depressed, and elated. She sometimes felt one or another and sometimes experienced several simultaneously. Pat's feelings were positive. She believed that her presence was valued: "I felt like they needed somebody there. The atmosphere was different. It seemed holy. It's traumatic, but not frightening. I try to be there." Liz verbalized a fatalistic and, perhaps, superficial attitude of acceptance: "God knocked on their door. What can I say? Everyone's slated. It's destiny." All agreed that they felt relief when it appeared that death ended the patient's suffering.

Most nurses admitted hesitancy in discussing death with a dying patient. Sandy stated, "It's never easy and there's never a set time. Both [patient and nurse] must be receptive." Amy said she speaks of death "only if they bring it up" and Barbara maintained:

They do more talking than I do. I listen and use reflection and other therapeutic techniques. It's easier with patients than with families. The families seem to have a more difficult time [accepting the impending death] than the patient.

Pat admitted that she never initiates this type of discussion, but takes "body language or eye contact as an initiative on the patient's part."

Katie believes that speaking with dying patients about their death is an integral component of hospice care, but not in each and every instance:

I don't mind [speaking with them]. They freak out initially, then are more concerned about family. Not all [patients] need to speak about it. I disagree with

Kubler-Ross—everyone dies differently as they live differently. Denial is okay if that's what they need to do.

This relates directly to the nurses' definitions of a "good death." Most nurses agreed that a good death varies for each patient, depending upon the values and needs of the patient. (Kubler-Ross (1970), in arguing that all individuals pass through certain predictable stages of dying, denies this individuality.) They did agree that an intrinsic need of the dying is to know they are not abandoned. The theme of loneliness again emerges.

How one performs as a nurse depends upon one's philosophy and values. If a nurse has learned to accept death and, more importantly, has learned to accept the fact that some individuals may accept death while others may fear it, she is better prepared to accompany her dying patients on their journey toward death.

The following description of one of the nurse's experiences with a patient at the moment of death poignantly reflects much more than an acceptance of death. It reflects an appreciation of life, of which death is the final part:

It became very still. Not quiet, but still. But it was as if a lot was happening. There was almost a presence felt in the room. And it wasn't bad. It felt calm, peaceful, and okay. No, it was more than okay. It was right and it was beautiful. And, all of a sudden, I felt the same kind of joyful tears that I felt when I saw my first baby born in nursing school. Then I realized that, at that very moment, [the patient] had died. Death seemed to be the same miracle as birth was.

Being present at the moment of death was, for this nurse, what Maslow (1972, pp. 48, 168–179) described as a "peak experience," a "transient moment of self-actualization." Peak experiences are personal events that are profound, joyous, blissful, transcendent, illuminating, mystical, and ecstatic; they result in feeling different about oneself or about the world. The experience described by this nurse, an experience triggered by a patient's death, contained these characteristics.

Peak experiences are, according to Maslow (1972), components of the self-actualization process, the process of becoming all we can be. Accompanying someone at the moment of death, a potential trigger for this type of experience, may be a powerful source of learning and of growth toward self-actualization.

Without denying that "this kind of work" is difficult, it is possible to experience it as an opportunity for personal growth.

Relationship of Beliefs to Observed Behavior

Values are expressed overtly through verbalization and covertly through norms and behavior. There was congruence between the observed behavior of the nurses on Four South and their expressed philosophies of nursing and personal values. Some examples of this congruence are illustrated in Table 1.

Table 1 Relationship of Nurses' Philosophies and Values to Their Observed Behaviors

Philosophy or Value	Observed Behavior
Barbara	
Listen to patients to provide support	Listened attentively to patients during rounds
Family needs to be included in care	Reassured wife of patient experiencing postoperative pain
Pat	
Help patients to verbalize feelings	Sought out patient to ask how things were going
Allow patient or family to initiate any discussion of death	Took cues from patient for discussion of her husband's terminal condition
Sandy	
The nurse acts as the patient advocate	Asserted herself with doctor in attempt to provide home care for patient
Katie	
Comfort is top priority	Medicated patient prior to his care in order to maintain his comfort
Make clergy available	Summoned priest for dying patient's family
Liz	
Provision of treatments is a nursing priority	Omitted diabetic teaching for patient because of involvement in physiological care and treatments for other patients
God controls one's destiny	Explained to patients that they are in "God's hands"
Sharon	
Patient education is a priority	Assessed patient's knowledge of nutritional components of her illness
Amy	
Comfort is top priority	Repositioned patient for optimal comfort
Patient has the right to care "given with a smile"	Smiled in genuine-looking way during care for patient when not enjoying that particular aspect of care

EXPRESSIVE AND INSTRUMENTAL BEHAVIORS

Expressive behaviors are those acts reported by the participant nurses themselves. Instrumental behaviors, or the actual behaviors of the participant nurses, are acts observed.

Expressive Behaviors

Nurses' behaviors on Four South were self-reported in two forms, oral and written. Written expression was found in nurses' notes, nursing care plans, or patient care classification units, while oral expression occurred either in conversation with other staff or in response to my questions.

Nurses' notes are written during each shift by the nurses caring for each patient. They are meant to be an objective description of the patient's status and are generated by observation, nursing actions designed to maintain or improve the patient's status, and by the patient's response to care. All hospitals, including MMC, adhere to this protocol.

Most nurses' notes reviewed were entirely limited to the physiological dimension of care. For example, one hospice chart was reviewed for a patient who had been on Four South for 22 days. The narrative nurses' notes for each of the three shifts for each of the 22 days were examined. The 66 notes devoted to this terminally ill patient documented pain control and respiratory status only. To judge solely by the notes, one would conclude that the patient's emotional and spiritual needs were totally ignored! Observation of the nurses caring for this patient, however, revealed that a great deal of emotional support was indeed provided for both the patient and his wife. Why, then, did the nurses omit documentation of this care?

Nurses at MMC utilize a special printed form for nurses' notes. The form provides labeled spaces for each type of documentation required and, on the reverse side of the form, room for narrative notes in excess of those in the labeled spaces. The form specifically provides space for intravenous therapy, hygiene, activities such as walking, diet, visits by physician and family, specimens obtained, treatments given, safety precautions used (e.g., siderails), and sleep habits. These labels elicit notes related to patients' physiological care. No space is provided for emotional or spiritual care. This may have tacitly communicated to the nursing staff that documentation in those two domains was unnecessary.

At MMC, as in all other hospitals, nurses write nursing care plans for each patient. These plans are designed to reflect actual and potential problems encountered by the patient in response to their illness, goals for each identified problem, and interventions designed to meet those goals.

Nurses on Four South were conscientious about having a care plan for each of their patients. On one particular day in which the patient census was 27, there were 23 care plans on record. Four patients had been admitted the previous evening and had not yet had their care plans written. In the 23 care plans, the problems identified pertained to pain, respiratory function, generalized anxiety, knowledge deficit, skin integrity, fluid and electrolyte balance, incontinence, and potential for injury. There were no identified problems relating to death and dying or to grieving, even for the six terminally ill patients among the 23. Of these six patients, five were well aware of their terminal status and were in varying stages of the dying process. The sixth patient was confused and, although she seemed to be unaware of her impending death, she was fearful.

Nurses caring for their patients consistently revealed their attention to patients' and families' anticipatory grief and fear related to the dying process. However, this attention was never mentioned in nursing care plans. As with the exclusion of certain types of care from written nurses' notes, one needs to question the reason for similar omissions from written nursing care plans.

Patient care classification units (PCCUs), the third vehicle for written self-expression of nursing behaviors, project staffing needs for the following shifts. Every morning each nurse completes a PCCU sheet, a checklist describing the amount and type of nursing care required for each of her patients. The number of nurses required for the next shift is determined on the basis of a formula applied to the classification sheet. The checklist is divided into several categories: diet, vital signs, toilet, cleanliness, medications and fluids, suctioning and respiration, transport, and isolation. Each category is broken down into subdivisions. For example, subdivisions for the vital signs category range from "BID," meaning twice daily, to "Q 1 H," meaning every hour.

The manner in which a nurse checks off the classification sheet reflects the amount of care required for her patients. Each item on the sheet is given a point value. One point is equivalent to 6.5 minutes of direct nursing care. Each day, points are totaled by each nurse to determine the total number of minutes of nursing care required for her patients. To each patient's points are added 14.5 minutes for "emotional support and teaching." Another 38 minutes are added for indirect care such as charting. There are no specific items for emotional or spiritual care or for patient teaching.

The PCCU system, like the form for nurses' notes, encourages documentation of care in the physiological domain only. Perhaps this was the reason that Four South nurses consistently failed to report, in writing, the emotional and spiritual care they provided for their patients.

Nursing behaviors were expressed orally either in conversation with other staff, as in the morning report session, or in direct response to my questions. An example of an orally expressed behavior in morning report occurred when Pat, Sandy, and Liz were discussing a patient who was upset because she "did not see a nurse from 10 p.m. to 3 a.m." and had been quite uncomfortable. Sandy stated, "I'll have Barbara go in and chat with her." Sandy followed through and requested Barbara to speak with the patient.

Another example of an orally expressed behavior occurred when Sandy, while waiting for morning report to begin, stated: "I usually don't get much out of that report, anyway. It takes forever and they really don't tell you what you need to know. I go in and look at and feel the patient. I talk to them. I get my info that way." Sandy was always observed to make morning rounds that included touching and speaking to each patient.

Instrumental Behaviors

Instrumental, or actual, behaviors were observed in all areas of Four South during the period of data collection. Observed behaviors of nurses were compared with reported behaviors to determine the relation between the two.

Relation of Expressive and Instrumental Behaviors

Orally expressed behaviors were congruent with instrumental behaviors in all observed interactions, whereas behaviors expressed in writing were incongruent with instrumental behaviors in that nurses reported, in writing, less than they had actually done.

For example, Mr. Brent, 62 years old and terminally ill with brain cancer, had been despondent over his poor prognosis, which he was just beginning to accept. Several nurses spent much time with both Mr. Brent and his wife in support of their emotional and spiritual needs. The nurses' notes on his chart, however, did not reflect the nursing activities performed. Instead, they reflected his physiological and mental status only; "confused; tried to get out of bed; placed in posey. Skin warm and dry to touch." There was no mention of the profound struggle Mr. and Mrs. Brent were having nor of the support offered by Mr. Brent's nurses.

Similarly, the nurses' notes for Mr. Kelly's care, like those for Mr. Brent, did not reflect the emotional and spiritual support offered by Katie for either Mr. Kelly, 69 years old and terminally ill with metastatic cancer, or for his wife. One morning, Katie explained her plan of care for Mr. Kelly: to give an injection of Thorazine to relieve his restlessness; wait 15 or 20 minutes until the Thorazine took effect and Mr. Kelly was comfortable; wash only his hands and face, as he was imminently terminal and a complete bath would only add to his stress; make him as comfortable as possible since "comfort is the priority"; not turn him, as turning would only add to his discomfort; not suction respiratory secretions although respirations were labored and noisy, because the fluids were so deep that suctioning would only alarm Mr. Kelly while decreasing his already low blood oxygen level.

This was exactly what Katie did 20 minutes following the injection of Thorazine. Her care was methodical, slow, and gentle. The only verbalization with Mr. Kelly was toward the end of his care:

Katie, RN: There. Is that more comfortable? . . . Isn't that better? [She kisses his forehead gently.]

Following Mr. Kelly's physiological care, Katie reported it exactly as it was planned and implemented. No mention was made, however, of the emotional support provided, the attempt to comfort, the touch, and the kiss.

Katie supported Mrs. Kelly both verbally and nonverbally. She provided support by shielding Mrs. Kelly from the unpleasant sight of her husband's draining secretions, making her aware that her presence was appreciated by her dying husband, praying with her, and remaining present.

The nurses' notes reflected none of this care. They were limited to physiological aspects of Mr. Kelly's condition: pulse, respirations, responsiveness. Nor did her oral report indicate any emotional support. It was as if this care was taken for granted; as if it was not necessary to document it, either orally or in writing.

Not all terminal care followed the pattern of Mr. Kelly's. Mrs. Fowler, 79 years old and imminently terminal, was Sharon's patient. Diagnosed with congestive heart failure, Mrs. Fowler had been completely unresponsive for several days. She had no family or significant other. Sharon was asked about her plan of care for Mrs. Fowler.

Sharon, RN: What d'ya mean?

Nelda: What are you going to do for her?

Sharon, RN: Oh. Wash her. The whole bit.

Sharon was extremely busy with other patients that morning. Every 15 or 20 minutes, however, she went to Mrs. Fowler's room to check on her to see if she was breathing. She repositioned Mrs. Fowler when she went in to check on her. Mrs. Fowler was alone for the greater part of the morning. When Sharon entered Mrs. Fowler's room to do her morning care, she bathed Mrs. Fowler completely, omitting nothing. Although Mrs. Fowler was unresponsive throughout, Sharon was extremely careful of how Mrs. Fowler was positioned during her care: "Let's be real quick so we can get her off her back. It's much harder for her to breathe on her back." Sharon was conscientious about Mrs. Fowler's skin care, massaging all bony prominences with lotion. When Sharon left the room, Mrs. Fowler was clean and comfortably repositioned, but alone. During one of her checks later in the morning, Sharon observed that Mrs. Fowler had stopped breathing, apparently without having regained consciousness.

Because Mrs. Fowler was completely unresponsive, Sharon maintained that she had no need for emotional or spiritual support during the last phase of dying. Mr. Kelly, in contrast, had been semiconscious and, although he was unable to respond verbally, it was perceived that he needed and appreciated emotional support. Additionally, Mrs. Kelly was present and needed this support, whereas Mrs. Fowler had no significant others present requiring this type of nursing care. Nursing care was adjusted to meet the perceived needs of patients and family, which is discussed in Chapter 5. Sharon reported care in the physiological domain. Nurses' notes and oral report of Sharon's actions were congruent with her nursing behavior.

Sandy's notes for Ms. Martin, the 42-year-old woman who underwent a mastectomy and received emotional support from both Sandy and Liz, reflected this care. The notes included all the physiological care provided, as well as a brief note describing Ms. Martin's emotional concerns, with a vague reference to care in that domain: "Patient concerned about discharge and being alone. Not prepared to look at surgical site. Teary and crying. Supportive therapy given."

INTERACTIVE BEHAVIORAL MODELS

The similar values articulated and enacted by the Four South nurses imply a shared attitude or ethos. As with any ethos, some participants model or typify the expressed ideals while others may be identified as marginal members.

Katie typified the majority of nurses on Four South. Her verbalized values indicated that meeting the patients' emotional and spiritual needs was of the highest priority, second only to their physical comfort. In most of Katie's observed interactions with patients, this philosophy was apparent. There were instances, however, when this philosophy was not apparent. For example, one of Katie's interactions with Mr. Brent ignored his references to his spiritual needs:

Mr. Brent: I've always gone to church regularly. While I'm not religious, I try. [Mr. Brent looks intently at Katie, waiting for a response.]

Katie, RN: [Changing the subject] How's your pain, Mr. Brent?

Katie was observed to interact in this manner during the times previously identified as being exceptionally busy for the nurses on Four South. These observations, like similar ones made of most of the other nurses, were the result of "busyness," a phenomenon discussed in detail in the next chapter.

Liz, while verbalizing ideals similar to the other participant nurses, can be identified as the most marginal of the group. Liz was observed to be more task-oriented than the rest of the group, focusing on such nursing interventions as administering medication, taking vital signs, and bathing. This was consistent with Liz's verbalized desire to have the time to "do more treatments."

Although Liz certainly spent time meeting the emotional and spiritual needs of her patients, she did so only after all their physiological needs, as she identified them, had been met. Liz put physiological care first in all observed interactions. For example, she was not able to meet an acutely ill patient's need for knowledge and reassurance by teaching the patient insulin self-administration because she was involved with the physiological needs of her other patients:

Liz, RN: Do you give your own insulin [at home]?

Mr. Moss: No, I've never had to.

Liz, RN: Then I'll come back later and give you the whole spiel.

However, Liz did not have the opportunity to return to Mr. Moss to teach insulin self-administration. Later in the day, as she passed his room, Mr. Moss called out to Liz from his room. Liz continued walking toward the nurses' station as she called back an answer, ignoring Mr. Moss' implicit request for reassurance that he was all right. At this moment, Liz's other patients had no immediate needs that had to be met; nevertheless, Mr. Moss's psychological need for knowledge and reassurance was ignored.

Observations of other participant nurses revealed that they placed the patient's emotional and spiritual needs above physiological needs that were not immediate. For example, Sandy and Amy were both observed to pause in their administration of medications to provide teaching or emotional support. While administering medication is necessary, both Sandy and Amy were observed to delay this task when they believed that a patient had immediate unmet emotional needs. Liz, who planned to return to her patients after her physiological interventions had been completed, frequently was unable to do so because all her time had been spent giving physiological care.

This does not mean that Liz never met patients' emotional or spiritual needs. In fact, Liz was often able to relate to the patients on Four South and to share her own personal experiences, which she was observed to do in her interaction with Ms. Martin. Liz's focus, however, was more on her patients' physiological needs than on their emotional or spiritual needs, in contrast with the focus of the other participant nurses.

ARE THESE NURSES DIFFERENT?

The hospice nurses observed in this study differed in several ways from nurses described in earlier studies (Gunther, 1977; Mandel, 1981). The nurses previously studied, all general duty nurses, were neither cognitively nor affectively prepared for their work. (See Gunther, 1977, and Mandel, 1981, for a discussion of past research related to nurses' care of the terminally ill.) The nurses on Four South were prepared cognitively for their specialized work with the dying through regular participation in continuing professional education related to the care of the terminally ill. They were affectively prepared to provide this care through regular attendance at their support group and through the development of a value system incorporating the concepts of life and death.

Philosophies of Life and Death

Unlike most nurses and, in all probability, most individuals in our society, each of the participant nurses had seriously thought about death, while confronting it every day and attending to those who experienced it. Each had given considerable thought to their philosophy of life and death and expressed feelings of acceptance of her own death. That is, they verbalized death as being non-threatening. This contrasts sharply with the nurses described in past studies who had not reconciled the concept of death in their own minds and felt threatened by it (Gunther, 1977; Mandel, 1981).

The nurses of Four South emphasized the application of their values and nursing philosophies in their nursing care. According to their verbalized nursing philosophies, however, they did not impose those values on their patients. As Amy stated, "Some [terminally ill] people just can't face [death] and I think that if they can't, they shouldn't have to." Although this was in direct conflict with what Amy wished for herself, she respected the wishes of some of her patients not to face their own death.

The nurses' personal feelings about death, however, may have caused some to make unconscious decisions that resulted in certain behaviors with dying patients. Although patients were viewed as unique individuals who were permitted to define their own "good death," some of the nurses' feelings may have influenced their behavior in the dying situation. For example, nurses who believed dying to be lonely would remain with their dying patients as long as possible.

This may explain, in part, why Sharon allowed Mrs. Fowler to die alone, whereas Katie remained with Mr. Kelly until the moment of death. Sharon believed that Mrs. Fowler, unresponsive during her last hours, did not need her presence. This belief was no doubt based on Sharon's own values, as Mrs. Fowler had not communicated her own wishes to Sharon. Katie remained with Mr. Kelly although he, like Mrs. Fowler, was unresponsive. She remained present to support Mrs. Kelly in her grief. This decision, too, was based on Katie's personal beliefs and values, as Mrs. Kelly had not requested Katie's presence, either verbally or nonverbally, although she did express her appreciation to Katie at a later time. The implication was that the nurses valued support, by way of personal presence, through the dying process only in instances where the person to be supported was responsive. The nurses assumed that unresponsiveness signified a lack of need for presence. Nurses, then, may contribute to a good death by meeting the individual patients' needs as they perceive them through the lens of their own personal value system. In other words, values or theories of practice guide patterns of behavior. Values are action-oriented, giving direction and meaning to one's life (Simon, 1973). They are reflected in patterns of behavior (Kluckhohn, 1955).

These findings are consistent with the literature on nursing values and philosophy. How one performs as a nurse depends upon one's philosophy (Uustal, 1978). Three concepts basic to nursing philosophy that serve as a guide to decision making include reverence for life, respect for the dignity and individuality of each person, and determination to act on one's beliefs (Wiedenbach, 1970). The Four South nurses described a reverence for life that included not only living, but dying, as well. Caring for the dying patient reflected their reverence for the living/dying process.

The "Good Nurse"

The idea of professional action based upon belief is consistent with the views of the "good nurse" by the nurses of Four South. A good nurse is willing to take risks for the benefit of the patient, the way Sandy did in her interaction with Dr. Norman. A good nurse attempts, as Liz did in her interaction with her unmarried, pregnant patient, to put aside her own biases so that patients' needs may be met. A good nurse, like Amy, is able to communicate a sense of concern to her patients even when that concern is not genuine.

Good nursing is an exacting role. Those who aspire to play the role well must cast aside their personal problems and biases before taking the stage. Only in this way can patients' needs be reliably met.

Distancing

Superficial analysis reveals that all of the participant nurses had similar feelings regarding death. However, a closer look reveals some differences. For example, Liz's use of clichés like, "It's destiny," in her discussion of death may be a distancing mechanism. It is understandable that Liz may have chosen to use distancing as a personal coping mechanism in view of her own health history.

Philosophical Similarities of Four South Nurses

Although the expressed values and philosophies of the participant nurses were not identical, the similarities were most striking. One naturally wonders how these similarities occurred. Several explanations are possible. It may be that certain values and beliefs arise from working on a daily basis with life and death. Values and beliefs, then, are affected by the work situation. Or it may be that the participant nurses have developed a deep bond after working together for more than five years and that this bonding has resulted in similar value systems. Or it may be that Four South nurses have come together and chosen their work based on pre-existing beliefs and values. I assume that there is interaction between past beliefs and values, the bonding mechanism occurring from prolonged involvement, and the work situation. Specific causes of a particular belief system cannot be isolated. Rather, they work together. Decisions and behaviors are based upon moral values, which are usually not of conscious choice (Burns, 1977, p. 77). These values, beliefs about what ought to be, are not identified as such and are usually acquired over a lifetime.

There is evidence to support the idea that pre-existing values are responsible for the type of work chosen by hospice nurses and that the unifying motivational theme of hospice nurses is a strong commitment to holistic care of the terminally ill. Pannier (1980) describes the major motivations for work in hospice. Hospice nurses have consciously chosen to care for the dying, after carefully examining their own beliefs and values related to living, dying, and death. This implies that, to care effectively for the dying, nurses must first examine their own philosophies of life and death (Burns, 1982).

These findings support earlier work by Hoggatt and Spilka (1979) describing the relationship of certain characteristics of nurses and the effects of those variables on the nurses' willingness to deal with dying patients. The variables included the nurses' personal attitudes toward death, the adequacy of their preparation in dealing with death and dying, and the frequency with which they dealt with terminally ill patients.

Nursing Priorities

Although the congruence between expressed values and philosophies of the Four South nurses was consistent with expectations based on the literature, it is reasonable to assume that all nurses' behaviors are not always consistent with their expressed ideals. The social and emotional aspects of care for terminally ill patients are viewed by most nurses as having top priority. In reality, however, medical and bureaucratic priorities often take precedence over expressed nursing priorities (Krantzler, 1980). This presents a discrepancy between the ideal and the actual role.

It is possible that Four South nurses had a unique opportunity to actualize their ideal role. General duty nurses are busier with the activities of acute care and the use of high technology. Their activities emphasize the curative aspect of care, whereas the hospice nurses on Four South were expected to prioritize their time differently. They were expected and permitted to utilize the limited commodity of time to help people die. Their hospice focus of care was emotional and spiritual in nature rather than physiological, although this focus was inconsistently reported by the nurses.

CONCLUSION

The nurses on Four South verbalized the development of personal philosophies and value systems that incorporated the concepts of life and death. Each of them, in her unique way, had come to accept the idea of death. Each, too, accepted the uniqueness of each patient along with each patient's right to define his or her own needs. These beliefs influenced not only the way the nurses lived their own lives, but the ways in which they cared for their patients.

LITERATURE CITED

Burns, N. (1982). *Nursing and cancer.* Philadelphia: W. B. Saunders.
Gunther, M. S. (1977). The threatened staff: A psychoanalytic contribution to medical psychology. *Comprehensive Psychiatry, 18,* 385–397.

Hoggatt, L., & Spilka, B. (1979). The nurse and the terminally ill patient: Some perspectives and projected actions. *Omega: The Journal of Death and Dying*, 9(3), 255–266.

Kluckhohn, F. R. (1955). Dominant and variant value orientations. In C. Kluckhohn & H. A. Murray (Eds.), *Personality in nature, society, and culture*. New York: Alfred A. Knopf.

Krantzler, N. J. (1982). Treatment for cancer: Nurses and the sociocultural context of medical care (Doctoral dissertation, University of California at Berkeley, 1982). *Dissertation Abstracts International*, 44, 212A.

Kubler-Ross, E. (1970). *On death and dying*. New York: Macmillan.

Mandel, H. R. (1981). Nurses' feelings about working with the dying. *American Journal of Nursing*, 6, 1194–1197.

Maslow, A. (1970). *Motivation and personality* (2nd ed.). New York: Harper & Row.

Maslow, A. (1972). *The farther reaches of human nature*. New York: Viking Press.

Pannier, E. A. The hospice care-giver: A qualitative study (Doctoral dissertation, Northwestern University, 1980). *Dissertation Abstracts International*, 41, 2456A.

Simon, S. B. (1973). *Meeting yourself halfway*. Niles, IL: Argus Communications.

Toynbee, A., & Koestler, A. (1976). *Life after death*. New York: McGraw-Hill.

Uustal, D. B. (1978). Values clarification in nursing: Application to practice. *American Journal of Nursing*, 12, 2058–2063.

Wiedenbach, E. (1970). Nurses' wisdom in nursing theory. *American Journal of Nursing*, 70(5), 1057–1062.

Chapter 5

Nursing the Living and the Dying

ACUTE AND TERMINAL LABELS

The major differences in the philosophical underpinnings of acute and terminal care were discussed in Chapter 1. In an effort to explore the similarities and differences in nursing interaction with these two mutually exclusive groups, Four South nurses' interactions with their acutely ill and terminally ill patients were compared. The constant comparison method of Glaser (1978) and Glaser and Strauss (1967) and the grounded-theory method described by Hutchinson (1986) and Wilson (1986, 1989) were used to compare nurses' interactions with both groups of patients. The comparison revealed two dimensions of nursing care: the biological and the psychospiritual.

Biological and Psychospiritual Care

Biological nursing care refers to the maintenance of activities of daily living such as personal hygiene and mobility, and to the implementation of nursing treatments. It involves technical care such as bathing and general assistance with hygiene, administration of medications, dressing changes, assistance with mobility, and physical assessment.

Spiritual care may fall within a religious, philosophic, or humanistic context. Most often, it is provided concurrently with psychological care. For this reason, the psychological and spiritual dimensions of care have been combined to form the *psychospiritual* dimension.

Psychospiritual nursing care is directed to the emotional and spiritual well-being of the patient. It includes assessment of the patient's psychological status and interventions designed to improve the status, as well as care directed toward assisting the patient to achieve his or her maximum potential as a human being. Some examples of nursing interactions in the psychospiritual domain are providing comfort and support to a patient who is anxious or upset; encouraging the expression of feelings; discussing the meaning of illness, life, and death with a patient; praying with a patient; showing affection and concern; and assisting with and supporting personal decisions. Although such interactions may occur during some aspect of biological care such as bathing, they are, nevertheless, intended to assess or improve the patient's psychological or spiritual status.

These two dimensions of care, biological and psychospiritual, were examined to identify their distinguishing characteristics within the domains of acute and terminal care.

Dimensions of Care with Acutely Ill Patients

Four South nurses often combined psychospiritual care with their biological care. Sandy discussed 67-year-old Mr. Young's medications with him, teaching him their side effects and explaining to him the cause of his nausea. She interacted in the biological dimension, discussing the clinical aspects of his medication regime.

Sandy, RN: [While handing the cup of medications to Mr. Young] How are you feeling today?

Mr. Young: Not so hot. I'm pretty nauseated. Been feeling like that since I started on this new pill. [He picks a green pill from the many in the medication cup.]

Sandy, RN: When did the nausea start?

Mr. Young: I was fine until a couple of hours after I took this. Then I really couldn't even stand to eat or drink anything.

Sandy, RN: Well, you know, it *is* possible that this is making you nauseous. It is one of the side effects and some people just can't tolerate it.

In this same observation, Sandy interacted in the psychospiritual dimension by supporting Mr. Young when he declared his reluctance to take a medication that sickened him.

Mr. Young: Well, I really would rather not take it again. [Places the pill back in the medication cup.] I'm really afraid that I'll throw up. And I feel so awful.

Sandy, RN: You know what I'm going to do? Watch this. I'm taking the pill with my fingers and getting rid of it. I'll check with your doctor to get something else for you.

Sandy interacted verbally by supporting his questioning of his medications, and nonverbally by disposing of the offending medication. She met his need for knowledge of his treatment by treating him as knowledgeable and well-informed health care consumer. Her expression of concern, too, was spiritually supportive, conveying a sense of caring.

Another example of a combination of biological and psychospiritual care was Amy's interaction with 64-year-old Mrs. Pizzo shortly after her abdominal surgery. With her arm around Mrs. Pizzo's shoulders, Amy assisted her into the bathroom. While Amy provided physical assistance, she maintained eye contact and listened intently to Mrs. Pizzo, thus providing psychospiritual care, as well.

At times, observed interactions with acutely ill patients were exclusively within the psychospiritual dimension. Liz responded exclusively in the psychospiritual dimension when she supported 42-year-old Ms. Martin's feelings of grief about her mastectomy. She showed Ms. Martin her own scar, told her how she felt when she had had the same surgery, and described how she had coped. Liz normalized Ms. Martin's crying by saying that it was natural and healthy for her to cry. In using her own mastectomy to assist Ms. Martin in accepting hers, Liz offered psychospiritual support and interacted exclusively in that dimension with this patient.

Both Liz and Sandy interacted verbally and nonverbally with Ms. Martin in this observation. Nonverbal interaction was observed from Sandy in the support offered by holding Ms. Martin's hand during the dressing change, a stressful procedure. Verbal interaction was observed as Sandy cried with Ms. Martin and when Liz assured Mr. Martin that "God is going to take good care of you."

Sandy's interaction with a 34-year-old patient recovering from abdominal surgery illustrates the use of touch and language in an interaction falling within both the biological and psychospiritual dimensions. While Sandy interacted verbally within the biological dimension, asking her patient about her bowel function, she gently touched the woman's foot. This touch conveyed intimacy and caring. Reinforcement of her patient's self-image was communicated through language when Sandy described the new suture line as "a real beauty."

On occasion, nurses interacted exclusively in the biological dimension with their acutely ill patients. For example, Sharon was caring for two women, one 69 years old and suffering from cholangitis, and the other 58 years old with a recent cholecystectomy. While changing an intravenous medication bottle and tubing, Sharon chatted amicably with both women about the nutritional aspects of their illnesses. Her conversation was factual and strictly limited to nutrition, while her attention was focused on the intravenous apparatus on which she was working.

With Mr. Moss, 67 years old and diabetic, Liz interacted entirely in the biological dimension when she responded to his inquiry about his blood pressure. Reading from her assignment sheet where she had recorded morning vital signs, Liz said in a factual manner: "Let's see. Your blood pressure this morning was 160/82. It's OK." Mr. Moss had been alone, confined to a chair in his room for most of the day. On this day, no one on the staff seemed to find the time to stop by his room to chat. Liz, apparently not perceiving Mr. Moss's question about his blood pressure as a call for attention or as an expression of a psychospiritual, or nonbiological, need, interacted with him in the biological dimension only.

Not surprisingly, the biological dimension, either alone or combined with the psychospiritual dimension, figured in nearly all observed interactions with acutely ill patients.

Dimensions of Care with Terminally Ill Patients

The biological dimension emerged in nearly all observed interactions with terminally ill patients as well. This was explained by Katie, who stated that "pain control and comfort are our priorities" on the hospice unit. Pain control and comfort fell within the biological aspect of patient care. According to Katie, patients' biological needs for safety and comfort must be met prior to meeting their psychospiritual needs. This is entirely consistent with Maslow's (1970) hierarchy of human needs.

In the care of terminally ill patients, biological care was usually combined with psychospiritual care, just as it was with acutely ill patients. There were occasions, however, when interactions took place exclusively in the biological or the psychospiritual dimension. An example of an interaction occurring exclusively in the biological dimension was the care Pat provided for unresponsive Mrs. Andrews, 79. Pat cared for her in silence, providing only biological care, that is, personal hygiene. Sharon, in caring for unresponsive 79-year-old Mrs. Fowler, also worked in silence, attending to her patient's hygiene and comfort. Sharon's care for Mrs. Fowler was time-consuming and thorough, as was Pat's care for Mrs. Andrews. In 25 minutes with Mrs. Fowler, Sharon attempted no verbal interaction with her unresponsive patient.

Psychospiritual interactions occurred in most observations of care provided to terminally ill patients. For example, Katie's interactions with Mr. and Mrs. Kelly included both biological and psychospiritual care. After gently completing Mr. Kelly' care, she demonstrated concern by kissing the unresponsive Mr. Kelly on the forehead. She supported Mrs. Kelly by assuring her of Mr. Kelly's comfort, encouraging her to remain in her husband's room, sharing in prayers, weeping, and comforting Mrs. Kelly following Mr. Kelly's death. Katie's nonverbal interaction with Mrs. Kelly included positioning her carefully at her husband's bedside during his last moments, being present at the bedside, protecting Mrs. Kelly from the unpleasant sight of her dying husband's bodily secretions, and allowing her some last moments of privacy with her husband following his death.

Pat, in interacting with Mrs. Vega, whose husband was terminally ill, provided psychospiritual care with her verbal support and advice: "The things that seemed important to you before won't be important anymore. Different things will matter." She also offered nonverbal support by holding hands and offering coffee.

Using touch and language, nurses on Four South interacted in similar ways with acutely ill and terminally ill patients within the biological and psychospiritual dimensions (Table 2). There were no apparent differences in the ways nurses interacted with their acutely ill and terminally ill patients. Other factors, however, did influence the ways nurses interacted with their patients. For example, the nurses' philosophies and values (discussed in Chapter 4) consistently influenced the way the nurses cared for their patients. The constantly changing dynamics of the unit also helped determine nurses' interactive behaviors.

UNIT DYNAMICS

On occasion, biological or psychospiritual care was conspicuously absent from a nurses' interactions with an acutely or terminally ill patient.

Inconsistencies

Katie's first interaction with Mr. Brent, 62 years old and terminally ill with metastatic brain cancer, took place primarily in the biological dimension. She introduced herself, discussed pain control, and offered suggestions regarding his diet. Mr. Brent touched on his spiritual concerns when he discussed seeing the chaplain and going to church regularly.

Mr. Brent: I've always gone to church regularly. While I'm not religious, I try. [Mr. Brent looks intently at Katie, waiting for a response.]

Katie, RN: [Changing the subject] How's your pain, Mr. Brent?

Mr. Brent: No pain. I'm great.

Katie, RN: I guess the pain medication is working. And that's why you're here.

In this interaction, Mr. Brent's cues for spiritual interaction with Katie remained undeveloped. (Psychological concerns were raised in the same exchange, when Mr. Brent spoke of his incurable illness.) Yet Katie continued to interact with Mr. Brent in the biological dimension, changing the subject after briefly mentioning control of the cancer.

This type of interactive behavior was inconsistent with the majority of observations, where interactions were well blended. Interactions that did occur

Table 2 Nursing Interactions Classified by Dimension of Care, Mode of Interaction, and Patient's Illness

Dimension/Mode of Interaction	Patient's Illness (and Degree of Responsiveness)		
	Responsive		Unresponsive or Confused
	Acute	Terminal	Acute or Terminal
Biological/verbal	Missed cue requesting psychospiritual support	Instructions to patient regarding help with care	Request to patient that nurse be allowed to wash her
	Asking about patient's physical state	Explanation about crushing pills	Command to patient to stop spitting
	Explaining side effects of medications	Information about home care	Explanation to patient about turning
	Asking about bowels and discussing discharge instructions	Information about skin care	
	Explaining about dressing change	Information to patient's wife on patient's condition and comfort	
	Assessing tolerance to diet	Information to patient's wife on what can be done for patient	
	Explaining about taking vital signs	Asking patient about pain, changing subject from psychospiritual	
	Instructions to remain in bed	Asking patient about breakfast, changing subject from psychospiritual	
	Discussing selection of diet	Introducing self	
	Asking how patient was feeling	Asking how patient was feeling	
	Giving patient information		

Table 2 Nursing Interactions Classified by Dimension of Care, Mode of Interaction, and Patient's Illness (Continued)

Dimension/ Mode of Interaction	Patient's Illness (and Degree of Responsiveness)		
	Responsive		Unresponsive or Confused
	Acute	Terminal	Acute or Terminal
Biological/tactile	Changing surgical dressing, with conversation Changing intravenous medication, with conversation Assisting patient from stretcher to bed, with conversation Taking patient's blood pressure, explaining Assisting patient to bathroom, with conversation Assisting patient to wash in bathroom, with conversation	Feeding patient through gastrostomy tube, eliciting participation Bathing patient in bed, while teaching about skin care Changing intravenous medication, with conversation Taking patient's vital signs, with conversation	Washing patient, with minimal verbal interaction at beginning of procedure Washing patient, with minimal verbal interaction to explain what was to be done Repositioning patient comfortably, in silence Bathing patient, in silence Repositioning patient, with a comment to patient Repositioning patient, in silence Bathing patient, with comments directed to researcher Medicating patient Bathing patient, making patient comfortable, in silence except for comment at end of procedure Taking patient's pulse, in silence

(Table continues on next page)

Table 2 Nursing Interactions Classified by Dimension of Care, Mode of Interaction, and Patient's Illness (*Continued*)

Dimension/ Mode of Interaction	Patient's Illness (and Degree of Responsiveness)			
	Responsive			Unresponsive or Confused
	Acute	Terminal		Acute or Terminal
Psychospiritual/verbal	Offer for patient to hold nurse's hand during stressful procedure	Assurance that patient will have help at home		Explanation that nurse is not "being mean" to patient
	Encouraging patient to express feelings after stressful procedure	Assurance that patients are discharged from unit		Asking, rhetorically, if patient is more comfortable
	Requesting presence of another nurse who could offer needed psychospiritual support to patient	Social conversation about books Advice to patient's wife about changing values		
	Crying with tearful patient	Support of patient's wife during patient's dying and death, including assurance that patient was comfortable, that wife's presence made a difference to patient, and praying with family		
	Sharing personal feelings with patient			
	Reassuring that patient is being taken care of by God			
	Supporting patient's reluctance to take medication that sickened him			
	Remark about "beauty" of surgical wound	Asking patient if there is anything they wanted to talk about		
	Comment, with smile, about eructation			
	Discussion and advice to patient about her personal life			
	Offering support to wife of patient in pain			
	Asking patient if there is anything they wanted to talk about			

Table 2 Nursing Interactions Classified by Dimension of Care, Mode of Interaction, and Patient's Illness (*Continued*)

	Patient's Illness (and Degree of Responsiveness)		
	Responsive		Unresponsive or Confused
Dimension/ Mode of Interaction	Acute	Terminal	Acute or Terminal
Psychospiritual/nonverbal	Holding patient's hand during entire duration of stressful procedure	Social conversation about where patient lives	Extremely gentle touch bathing
	Throwing of breast prosthesis on table for patient to see	Shaking hands with patient	Omission of unnecessary care that would add to patient's stress
	Disposing of medication in support of patient's reluctance to take it	Holding patient's hand	
	Touching patient's foot, smiling, and maintaining eye contact during conversation	Maintaining eye contact when giving reassurance	
	Listening, with smile, to patient's conversation	Providing coffee for patient's wife	
	Hugging patient who is having difficult time with a personal decision	Holding patient's wife's hands while speaking with her	
	Giving patient undiviced attention	Remaining present with patient's family during dying process and death, shielding family from unpleasant sight	
	Shaking hands with patient		
	Holding patient's hand		

exclusively in one or the other dimension of care usually arose in response to specific patient needs. (An example was Liz's interaction with Ms. Martin.)

When nurses were extremely busy, as Katie was at the time of her first interaction with Mr. Brent, they tended to focus more readily on the biological dimension, regardless of whether their patient was acutely or terminally ill. On the day of this particular interaction Four South was unusually busy. There were 33 patients, 11 of whom were terminally ill and required extensive nursing care. Katie, in particular, was busy. With the assistance of one nurse's aide, she was responsible for the care of eight patients, three of whom were terminally ill. Three others were scheduled for surgery that morning and thus required additional preparatory work. In addition, Katie had been off for several days and did not know her patients or their specific needs.

That same morning Liz, like Katie, was quite busy with her assignment. Liz's interactions with Mr. Moss took place entirely in the biological dimension, as she responded to his question about his blood pressure but not to his covert request for attention. Lack of familiarity with patients, combined with an increased amount of work, appeared to result in a biological focus of care, regardless of whether a patient was acutely or terminally ill.

The particular "busyness" engendered in the nurses under such circumstances had a direct impact on the ways the nurses interacted with their patients. Normally, patients received holistic nursing care designed to meet all their needs. Busyness affected the focus of care.

"Busyness"

A nurse's busyness, which reduces the amount of time she has to spend on patient care, may be affected by several variables. The number of patients on the unit on a given day is directly related to the number of patients for which each nurse is responsible. The type of care required by patients also affects the amount of time needed for their care. For example, patients who are physically or psychologically unstable require more extensive nursing care than stable patients. Patients unable to care for themselves require more nursing care than patients who meet their own needs. Changes in the patient population thus affect the amount of time nurses have to spend providing care for each member of that population.

Like patient characteristics, staffing patterns also affect the nurses' work. Staffing patterns on Four South changed on a daily basis. The number of nurses working on the unit depended on variables such as nurses' vacations, their personal days off, and absences due to illness. If possible, substitutes were found for absent nurses. Even when available, however, the replacement nurses sent to Four South were not able to function in the same manner as the nurses who regularly staffed the unit and knew the unit's routine. More important, replacements were unfamiliar with the patients on Four South and with their specific needs.

Changes in staffing patterns and in patient population, often made it necessary to shift nursing assignments, increasing the likelihood of a nurse being assigned to care for a group of patients with whom she was unfamiliar.

Each of these variables—patient census, patients' characteristics, staffing patterns, and familiarity with assigned patients—affected the busyness of the nurses. The busier a nurse was, the less time she had to assess her patient's needs and to design care to meet those needs. When less time was available, nurses necessarily prioritized their care and concentrated on those facets of care deemed most important. On days when nurses were observed to be quite busy, the focus of nursing care and of nurse-patient interaction was primarily biological.

Unlike certain variables discussed in Chapter 4 (personal biases and interpersonal relations among the nurses), which did not appear to affect the level and quality of nursing care, busyness was observed to change the focus of nurse-patient interactions.

Focus of Care in Hospice

While the focus of acute care is on the biological dimension to support the goal of maintaining life and preventing death, hospice care is designed to focus equally on the biological, psychological, and spiritual dimensions of the individual. Although physical comfort is a priority of terminal care and, as such, falls within the biological dimension, equal emphasis is given to the patient's psychological and spiritual dimensions (Burger, 1980; Dobratz, 1990; Samarel, 1988; Schraff, 1988; Young & Jacobs, 1983).

The absence of one or the other dimension of interaction in particular observations appears to conflict with the holistic nature of hospice care. Because factors such as nurses' values, philosophies, and the degree of busyness on the unit affected nursing care, it is apparent that a generalization about the focus of nursing care for hospice patients on Four South cannot be universally valid.

DIFFERENCES AMONG INDIVIDUAL NURSES

Although there were no observed differences in the ways each nurse interacted with acutely ill and terminally ill patients, there were differences between nurses in interactive behaviors. Some nurses were more likely than others to combine interactions in all dimensions.

For example, Sandy, interacting simultaneously in the biological and psychospiritual dimensions, treated terminally ill Mrs. Archer no differently than she treated acutely ill Mr. Young. She used her time with each of them to teach and to support.

Nor did patient age make a difference in Sandy's interactions. As Sandy administered medications to her 34-year-old patient, acutely ill with recent surgery for removal of an ovarian cyst, she stood next to the bed conversing, smiling, maintaining eye contact, and gently touching the woman's foot—all psychospiritual interactions. Interacting in the biological dimension, she asked about her patient's bowels, promised to check the laxative order, and discussed discharge instructions. Later, while changing the woman's surgical dressing, she explained exactly what she was doing. Then, pointing to the suture line, she remarked on what a "beauty" it was. Sandy responded to her patient's psychological need to maintain a positive body image while she provided physical care.

Sharon's observed verbal interactions during direct nursing care with both acutely and terminally ill patients were formally limited to the biological dimension. Sharon used the same casual, chatty method of assessment with terminally ill Mrs. Hunt, 68 (see pages 49–51), as she did with acutely ill Mr. Sharpe, 37 (see pages 51–52). Although her overt behavior appeared to be mainly within the biological dimension, Sharon was observed to interact with her patients, if somewhat covertly, in the psychospiritual dimension. Sharon's nonverbal behavior, such as eye contact and concerned facial expression, was psychologically and spiritually supportive to her patients.

Most observed verbal interactions between Amy and her acutely and terminally ill patients occurred within the biological dimension. For example, Amy asked terminally ill Mr. Richards, 54, about his seemingly relentless pain.

Amy, RN: [Standing next to Mr. Richards's bed] How's the pain?

Mr. Richards: Oh, it's much better now. But the fear is still there. [In a shaky voice filled with fear] I know it's coming back. It always does and I'm not sure how much more I can stand it.

Amy, RN: [Looking very concerned, putting down her patient chart and pulling a chair to Mr. Richards's bedside] Let's see, I medicated you about 30 minutes ago. Let's not wait until the pain comes back. If I medicate you again in about 2½ hours, before this medication wears off, perhaps we can prevent it from coming back. [Looks at Mr. Richards for a response.]

Mr. Richards: Do you really think that will help?

Amy, RN: [Taking Mr. Richards's hand] Yes, I do. And it's certainly worth a try.

Amy's nonverbal behavior—eye contact, facial expression, and touch—was, like Sharon's, psychologically and spiritually supportive to her patients.

RESPONSIVENESS VERSUS UNRESPONSIVENESS, OR DO THEY NEED ME?

Nurses interacted and made decisions on the basis of their assessment of patient needs and not on whether the patient was terminally ill or acutely ill. However, they did interact differently with responsive patients than with patients who were unresponsive (Table 2).

Interactions with Responsive Patients

Sandy used her time with her acutely ill 37-year-old patient to assess her patient's knowledge about her recent abdominal surgery, to reassure, and to teach. Her interactions combined physical care and emotional support, especially in helping to restore a positive body image for this patient. Sandy's interaction with terminally ill Mrs. Archer, 73 years old and paralyzed with amyotrophic lateral sclerosis, also involved assessment, reassurance, and teaching.

Upon entering Mrs. Archer's room with medications, Sandy slowly and patiently explained exactly what she was doing: "Now I'm going to crush these pills and feed them to you [through the feeding tube] with your feeding. You can't swallow them and this is really the same. It's an easy way to take them [as she crushed the pills].

Sandy then started the gastrostomy feeding. When Mrs. Archer verbalized concern about her ability to be cared for at home, Sandy was reassuring: "I'll arrange for nurses at home. I'll call social service and the visiting nurse service. You *will* go home with the proper help. People do go home from here, you know."

A while later, when Sandy was bathing Mrs. Archer, the two were chatting about Mrs. Archer's family, the books she was reading, and the condition of her skin, an important issue as Mrs. Archer was immobile and prone to skin breakdown. Sandy maintained eye contact with Mrs. Archer during much of the conversation.

Like most of her colleagues, this nurse's interaction with two responsive patients, one terminally ill and the other acutely ill, included teaching, reassurance, and social conversation with eye contact throughout each interaction.

Interactions with Unresponsive Patients

Terminally ill Mr. Steele, 72 years old, was unresponsive to verbal stimuli and moaned continuously. As Sandy and a nurse's aide worked together bathing him, they worked gently, quickly . . . and silently. Sandy commented to the aide at one point that she did not understand why Mr. Steele was moaning, as she had medicated him only 30 minutes earlier. When his care was completed, they repositioned Mr. Steele on his side. He stopped moaning. Before Sandy left the room, she patted Mr. Steele on the head and said to him, "There now. Isn't that more comfortable for you?"

Sandy's interactions with Mrs. Archer and Mr. Steele differed. Although Sandy's gentle style of caring was evident with both terminally ill patients, her care for unresponsive Mr. Steele was given with no teaching, social conversation, reassurance, or eye contact. In responding to whether or not her patients could communicate, Sandy's behavior was consistent with that of her colleagues.

An example of a nurse's interactions with an unresponsive and imminently terminal patient was Sharon's interactions with 79-year-old Mrs. Fowler. During the morning report one hour earlier, Sharon stated that she did not think Mrs. Fowler would live through the morning. Shortly thereafter, Sharon provided complete physical care for Mrs. Fowler. Mrs. Fowler was unresponsive throughout, moaning occasionally as Sharon repositioned her. No verbal interaction between the two occurred during the entire 25-minute procedure. When Sharon left the room, she left Mrs. Fowler positioned comfortably, resting quietly . . . and alone.

Sharon's caring for Mrs. Fowler was similar to Sandy's observed style with Mr. Steele. Sharon was gentle, thorough, concerned with Mrs. Fowler's comfort, and, like Sandy, silent.

Four South nurses were observed to care for patients in silence only when the recipients of the care were unresponsive. Physical care for these patients was provided in a gentle and caring way. Speech was limited to the nurses' rhetorical questions, such as the one Sandy addressed to Mr. Steele.

All Four South nurses provided the physical care needed by their unresponsive patients. In informal conversations with me they discussed their beliefs that these unresponsive patients needed no verbal interaction. Their comments included the following:

She doesn't even know I'm here.

It's a blessing he's out of it.

I guess it doesn't matter [if I don't speak to her] because she doesn't know the difference.

Four South nurses believed that little emotional or spiritual support was needed for unresponsive patients. Consequently, they limited their care to touch and gentle handling.

Interactions with Disoriented Patients

Four South nurses were observed to interact differently with disoriented patients as well. (A disoriented patient is in a state of mental confusion, often characterized by inaccurate perceptions of identity, place, or time.) Liz interacted differently with two 79-year-old acutely ill patients. Mrs. Tower was alert and oriented, whereas Mrs. Ray was confused, nonverbal, and often combative.

Liz initiated a social conversation with Mrs. Tower, who was capable of participating in such a conversation. The two chatted while they busied themselves with their tasks, Mrs. Tower washing herself and Liz making the bed.

There was no such interaction with Mrs. Ray. Liz told me that she believed her patient's behavior was unalterable in that she was generally "combative" and that the best thing to do was to quickly complete her care and "not bother her any more than necessary." Liz washed Mrs. Ray in silence as Mrs. Ray tried to push Liz's hands away.

Liz, RN: You act as if I'm being mean to you. I'm not being mean to you.

She then continued to work quickly with no attempts at further communication. Mrs. Ray lay in silence, watching Liz's every move with a wary look on her face, saying nothing.

The difference in Liz's interactions with two acutely ill patients was based upon her stated perception of their orientation and of their abilities to respond. No attempts were made to communicate in any meaningful way with disoriented Mrs. Ray. There was no conversation, as there was for the patient who was alert and oriented.

Interactions with the Dying

Nurses' beliefs about their responsive and unresponsive patients' needs also affected the type of support given during the dying process. For example, Sharon provided meticulous care in a gentle and concerned way for imminently terminal, unresponsive Mrs. Fowler. This care, requiring 25 minutes, was done in silence. When it was completed, Sharon repositioned Mrs. Fowler comfortably and left the room. She returned at regular intervals to "see if she was still breathing." Later in the morning, Mrs. Fowler had, indeed, stopped breathing. She was left alone during most of the dying process and was alone, too, at the moment of death. After all, though, "She doesn't even know I'm here." This same nurse, however, remained with another imminently terminal patient, who was responsive through the final stages of the dying process, indeed until the moment of death.

Eighty-two-year-old Mrs. Simon had been admitted repeatedly for metastasized cancer. Now, her cancer was out of control and Mrs. Simon was back on Four South in her terminal admission. This morning, she lay back in bed, pale and weak, barely able to speak. Her breath was shallow and her eyes were tired. Sharon was sitting on the side of the bed brushing the hair off Mrs. Simon's cool, damp forehead.

Mrs. Simon: I'm really tired. [Sighs.]

Sharon, RN: It's been a long haul for you.

Mrs. Simon: Yes [her voice a whisper].

Sharon, RN: I'll just sit here with you.

Mrs. Simon: [Silently reaches for Sharon's hand.]

Mrs. Simon died quietly several minutes later, her hand still in Sharon's.

When patients were responsive, nurses remained with and supported them throughout the dying process. Patients who were unresponsive, however, were permitted to die alone. As the comments cited earlier demonstrate, nurses believed that unresponsive patients did not require their presence. This implied that the nurses valued personal support through the dying process only in instances where the dying patient was responsive.

Although patients' unresponsiveness signified to the nurses their lack of need for emotional support, an interesting exception was observed when patients' families were present, at which times the nurses attempted to remain throughout the dying process to support the families in their grief. For example, Katie remained with unresponsive Mr. Kelly during the last stages of the dying process. She supported Mrs. Kelly during this difficult time through verbal reassurance, comfort, and understanding, as well as through her physical presence.

The nurses expressed their beliefs that, although unresponsive dying patients needed minimal or no personal interaction, their families needed support through the dying and the death. In addition to providing direct emotional support for families, the nurses remained present so that family members could see that their dying loved one was being cared for. Consequently, unresponsive patients whose family members were present were attended to in ways similar to responsive patients.

SYMBOLIC INTERACTIONISM:
AN EXPLANATORY FRAMEWORK

Four South nurses assessed the needs of their patients. Their assessments were based on what they saw and heard—on the gestures and speech of each patient—and not on the basis of the patient's status as acute or terminal. Rather than responding to their patients' medical prognoses, nurses responded to what their patients said and did. On the basis of the perceived meaning of these acts, the nurses responded by interacting or not interacting in a particular manner.

The interactionist perspective for viewing behavior was described by Blumer (1969). In an interactionist perspective, most situations are unique. There are few universals or generalizations. Interactive behaviors are not based upon artificial categories or boundaries such as those that might be established between terminally ill and acutely ill patients. Priorities of care vary with each individual patient, depending on their level of consciousness or orientation, which nurses believe to determine the patient's needs.

CONCLUSION

It was surprising that neither a terminal diagnosis nor imminent death was central in determining the ways Four South nurses interacted with their patients. There were no differences in the care given by any one nurse to acutely ill or terminally ill patients. If a nurse had the quality of compassion, that quality was used in the care of all her patients.

Although the nurses interacted with all their patients, interactive behaviors diminished in the care of unresponsive and disoriented patients. In those interactions, nursing behaviors were predominantly nonverbal and limited to gentle touch when physical care was being given. Priorities of care varied for each patient, depending on their responsiveness and orientation, which the nurses believed to determine their needs.

Although each of the nurses had given considerable thought to the issue of death and could describe her own notions of a "good death," as discussed in Chapter 4, this was not apparent in some interactions with patients. The nurses dealt with the dying process differently for responsive and unresponsive patients because they believed that their unresponsive patients' needs during the dying process differed from the needs of their responsive patients; only the latter were believed to need the nurses' presence to effect a "good death." Unresponsive patients whose families were present, however, were tended to in the same manner as responsive patients. The nurses believed that, although the unresponsive patients needed little verbal interaction and support, their families did.

LITERATURE CITED

Blumer, H. (1969). *Symbolic interactionism.* Englewood Cliffs, NJ: Prentice-Hall.

Burger, S. (1980). Three approaches to patient care: Hospice, nursing homes, and hospitals. In M. Hamilton & H. Reid (Eds.), *A hospice handbook: A new way to care for the dying,* p. 132. Grand Rapids, MI: Eerdmans.

Dobratz, M. C. (1990). Hospice nursing: Present perspectives and future directives. *Cancer Nursing,* 13(2), 116–122.

Glaser, B. G. (1978). *Theoretical sensitivity.* Mill Valley, CA: Sociology Press.

Glaser, B. G., & Strauss, A. L. (1967). *The discovery of grounded theory: Strategies for qualitative research.* New York: Aldine.

Hutchinson, S. (1986). Grounded theory: The method. In P. L. Munhall & C. J. Oiler (Eds.), *Nursing research: A qualitative perspective,* pp. 111–130. Norwalk, CT: Appleton-Century-Crofts.

Maslow, A. (1970). *Motivation and personality* (2nd ed.). New York: Harper & Row.

Samarel, N. (1988). Caring for life and death: Nursing in a hospital-based hospice (Doctoral dissertation, Rutgers University, 1987). *Dissertation Abstracts International,* 48, 2607B.

Schraff, S. H. (1988). *The hospice concept.* New York: National League for Nursing.

Wilson, H. S. (1986). Presencing—Social control of schizophrenics in an antipsychiatric community: Doing grounded theory. In P. L. Munhall & C. J. Oiler (Eds.), *Nursing research: A qualitative perspective,* pp. 131–144. Norwalk, CT: Appleton-Century-Crofts.

Wilson, H. S. (1989). *Research in nursing.* Redwood City, CA: Addison-Wesley.

Young, D., & Jacobs, A. M. (1983). *Hospice nursing: A model curriculum for continuing education.* Los Angeles: California State University.

Chapter 6

Role Transition: How Do the Nurses "Change Gears"?

ROLE THEORY

A brief exploration of role theory will help readers understand and appreciate the way nurses "change gears" to care for their acutely and terminally ill patients, the way they meet the needs of these two groups.

Nurse-patient interaction is an essential component of the nursing role. Nursing is a therapeutic, goal-oriented, interpersonal process with nurse-patient interactions initiated in relation to patient needs as these are perceived by the nurse. Needs may be biological, psychological, or spiritual in nature and will differ with varying health problems, as will the nurses' perceptions of these needs. For further discussion of nursing roles, see American Nurses' Association (1976), Brodish (1982), and Peplau (1952). May (1990) has reviewed the literature on nurse-patient relationships.

Role theory can be used to predict how individuals will behave or act in a given situation or role. Conway (1978) describes two major perspectives to the study of role theory. The functionalist perspective is physically oriented and based on the assumption that an individual's role in society is fixed. Functionalism focuses on objects and actions as stimuli that elicit responses from individuals. The interactionist perspective, or symbolic interactionism, maintains that an individual's actions are responses to the symbolic acts, in the forms of speech and gestures, of others. The perspective of this inquiry was interactionist.

According to the interactionist perspective, our responses are based upon our interpretations of others' acts. Our interpretations are dependent upon our personal philosophy and value system. Symbolic interactionism explains behavior through the meaning and value of personal experiences.

Meeting the needs of two separate and distinct patient populations within a single setting may require registered nurses to make role transitions. Role transition occurs naturally when a nurse leaves the work setting and resumes the role of spouse, child, or parent. It occurs when a patient leaves the hospital and resumes the role of parent or teacher.

The two problems commonly associated with role transition are role insufficiency and role conflict. Role insufficiency, the actor's self-perception of inadequate role performance, may be caused by poorly defined roles or inadequate knowledge of role behaviors and goals, resulting in guilt about the deficit between role performance and personal role expectations (Meleis, 1975). This problem may be experienced by nurses who believe that their work situation did not allow them to meet the needs of the dying (Williams, 1982). Role insufficiency may be prevented or relieved by role supplementation, which strengthens role function through role modeling or reference groups such as consultations or peer group discussions (Meleis, 1975).

When role transition encompasses contradictory or mutually exclusive role expectations, the problem of role conflict is encountered (Hardy, 1978). The hospice nurse is expected to fight death in the acutely ill while caring for the dying. The hospice setting, containing patients whose care needs are so disparate, may render any universal view of nursing ambiguous. Do the disparate concepts in the inpatient hospice result in contradictory role expectations or role conflict for hospice nurses?

As noted in Chapter 1, a similar potential for role conflict resulting from attempts to meet differing needs of two patient populations confronts obstetrical nurses who care for patients experiencing induced abortions. Indeed, role ambiguity, conflict, and incongruity are problems faced by teachers (Caplan & Jones, 1975), physicians (Lennard & Bernstein, 1966; Overall & Aronson, 1966), social workers (Scott, 1969), and other professionals (Miles, 1975; Snoek, 1966), as well as by other nurses (Arndt & Laeger, 1970; Corwin, 1961; Kramer, 1968).

DISPARATE IDEOLOGIES OF CARE

This research was focused on the role transition required of a group of nurses in a hospital-based discrete hospice unit. Nurses in such a setting operate under dichotomous ideologies of care. As shown in Table 3, hospice and acute care ideologies differ in views of death, priorities for nursing care, focus of unit of care, pain management philosophies, and goals of care (Burger, 1980; Samarel, 1988, 1989a; Young & Jacobs, 1983). A discrete, inpatient, hospital-based hospice contains patients whose care needs are disparate. Reconciling these needs may be difficult for health care professionals working in such a setting, creating a risk of role insufficiency and role conflict.

Role Insufficiency

The nurses on Four South verbalized no feelings of role insufficiency. I hypothesize that this was due to the fact that the nurses had a strong hospice identity and had been thoroughly prepared for their role through attendance at continuing professional education offerings related to the care of the terminally ill. Their goals of care were continually discussed among themselves, informally in conversation and more formally at the morning report. They received role supplementation in multiple ways. Their support group meetings, discussions with hospice team members, conversations among themselves regarding patient care, and role modeling for each other all served to prevent role insufficiency.

Role Conflict

If disparate roles share a unifying focus, they may be reconciled with no role conflict. My analysis of the kinds of nursing care I observed led me to explore the concept of care in nursing and to examine the literature on caring (see Appendix C). Caring was the unifying thread that allowed the nurses of Four

Table 3   Ideologies of Care

Concept	Hospice View	Acute Care View
Death	Natural Accepted	Failure Denied
Goals of care	Comfort Palliation Assist with dying process Maintain quality of life	Prolong life Curative Prevent death Survival
Priorities of care	Comfort Equal emphasis on physical, psychological, and spiritual care Family-centered	Survival Primary emphasis on physical care Family involvement is usually peripheral
Term of care	Extends past patient's death to include bereavement	Ends with patient's death or discharge

See Burger (1980) and Young and Jacobs (1983) for more discussion of this topic.

South to reconcile the intentions of hospice and acute care without role conflict (Figure 2).

NURSING AS CARING

Several themes appeared throughout the nurses' discussions and were consistently reflected in their observed actions. These themes included empathy, compassion, concern, sensitivity, and faith. All are generally associated with caring (Leininger, 1981; Watson, 1979), which I define as the facilitation of growth toward wholeness in another who is in need of this help.

Caring Strategies

Nurses were observed to use caring strategies when attempting to meet their patients' needs. Some examples of nurses' use of caring strategies with acutely ill and terminally ill patients follow.

Sandy and Liz were observed in an interaction with acutely ill Cindy Martin, 42 years old and newly diagnosed with breast cancer. She had had a mastectomy three days earlier. Ms. Martin's doctor spent 15 minutes with her, redressing the operative site, explaining the exercises she was to do with her

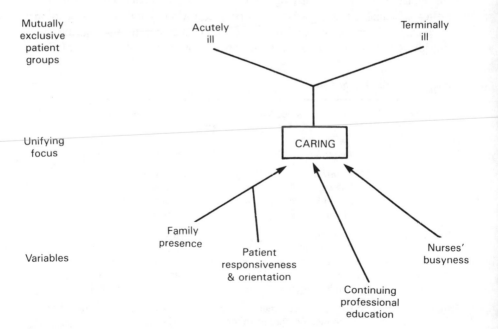

Figure 2 Linkage of patient groups, unifying focus, and variables.

affected arm, and reinforcing the fact that she had had a malignancy. When the doctor left the room, Ms. Martin spoke to Sandy.

Ms. Martin: I thought I was gonna cry when he took off the dressing.

Sandy, RN: How do you feel now that he spoke to you?

Ms. Martin: Relieved. At least now I know [that I have cancer].

She then started to cry. Sandy immediately summoned Liz into Ms. Martin's room, having decided that Liz was best able to offer the emotional support Ms. Martin needed because Liz too had had a mastectomy and could relate to Ms. Martin's feelings.

Liz entered the room as Ms. Martin was tearfully telling Sandy that she could never accept the mastectomy. Sandy, too, was crying. Liz moved officiously across the room to the table where Sandy and Ms. Martin were crying and, without a word, removed her own breast prosthesis and threw it on the table in front of Ms. Martin. With that, all three women burst into laughter. Ms. Martin commented that she had been unaware that Liz had also had a mastectomy. Liz showed Ms. Martin her scar, told her how she felt when she had had her surgery, and described how she had coped. She supported Ms. Martin by saying that it was natural and healthy to cry.

Liz admittedly used a brash, direct, and surprisingly humorous approach to relieve the tension in the room. This was followed by gentle support and verbalized understanding. Ms. Martin later spoke of Liz as a "great source of comfort" to her.

In this instance, the nurses assessed the patient's needs based on what was seen and heard, on the gestures and speech of the patient, rather than on the basis of an imposed label of "acute" or "terminal." Caring was evident in the way Sandy used available resources, that is, in summoning another nurse whose personal experience could be offered to support the patient. Caring was also evident in the manner in which Liz used "normalizing" as a strategy of support for a tearful patient who was grieving the loss of her breast.

In another example, Katie used caring strategies with Mr. Kelly, 69 years old, unconscious, and imminently terminal with metastatic cancer. Mr. Kelly's respirations were labored and noisy and he was quite restless, although he was receiving morphine via continuous intravenous drip. Katie medicated Mr. Kelly and waited 20 minutes before beginning his physical care. This allowed the medication to take effect and relieve his restlessness. Katie's care was slow, methodical, and gentle. She made Mr. Kelly as comfortable as possible, positioning him in high Fowler's position to facilitate his breathing. Toward the end of his care, Katie spoke to the unconscious Mr. Kelly: "There. Is that more comfortable? . . . Isn't that better?" She then kissed his forehead gently, reflecting her compassion and caring.

Caring was reflected, too, when Katie admitted that, at times, it was difficult to do "this kind" of work. "Sometimes we laugh a lot. But it relieves tension. And sometimes I think I just don't feel anything anymore. But then I find myself crying for no apparent reason." The patient who precipitated these comments was Judy Palumbo, a 37-year-old woman, terminally ill with cancer and in great pain when awake. Katie stated that a few days earlier she and a doctor had entered Judy's room and found her pain to be "out of control." She screamed and clawed at Katie, who described it as "a horrible experience." The doctor administered an intravenous sedative. As he did so, Katie held both of her patient's hands in her own and tried to reassure her in a firm voice, "It will be OK, Judy. It will be OK in a minute." Katie released Judy's hands only after the woman was deeply asleep.

At the nurses' station a while later, Katie again spoke about this patient's pain. As she spoke, her thumbs moved agitatedly back and forth against the rings of the looseleaf binder she held and a tear rolled down her cheek.

The strength of the caring aspect of the Four South nurses' professional behaviors was consistently demonstrated. Their caring was apparent in the ways they interacted with their patients, striving to show believable concern, attending to needs within time constraints, and attempting to demonstrate their understanding of the patients' situations. It was also apparent in the discussions between the nurses. For example, several nurses verbalized their concern for the daughter of a terminally ill patient. They assessed, identified, and acted on their perception of the daughter's need for relief from the ongoing care of her father. This type of nursing went beyond the physical care provided to the identified patient, the terminally ill father.

Caring was apparent, too, in the nurses' discussion of Mr. Taylor, 76 years old, semiconscious, and imminently terminal with lung cancer. At one point he had become increasingly restless and apprehensive, and his pain was unrelieved by injections. He was comfortable only with a morphine drip, which had been in place for the past 24 hours. When the hospice coordinator, acting on doctor's orders, replaced the morphine drip with dextrose, Amy became visibly upset. She and Sandy discussed what could be done if Mr. Taylor became uncomfortable and how an order for the morphine drip could be obtained. The conversation then turned to the doctor's reluctance to utilize morphine to make a terminal patient comfortable. The two nurses discussed ways in which a nurse may manipulate a physician into ordering medication for a patient and the guilt that accompanied such manipulation. Amy commented rhetorically, "Well, does the patient benefit? That's the bottom line. You do whatever you have to do so that the patient will benefit." Sandy agreed that nurses were indeed the patients' advocates and that they must do everything they can to ensure that the patient gets needed care.

Caring was evident in the nurses' concerns for Mr. Taylor's comfort. Caring was also evident in the calls they made in an effort to obtain an order to restart the morphine drip.

Humanistic caring, caring *about* the patients, was the unifying focus of the care provided to acutely and terminally ill patients on Four South. It formed the core of the shared values and nursing philosophies of the nurses in the hospice unit. The following sections examine caring as an explanation of the findings of this study, explore the relationship of symbolic interactionism and caring, and investigate the effect of busyness on caring behaviors.

Caring as an Explanation of Findings

Past research has shown that nurses caring for the terminally ill attempt to protect themselves by developing a callous exterior (Benoliel, 1974; Pillette, 1980) and by assuming attitudes of exaggerated detachment (Pattison, 1978; Glaser & Strauss, 1979). The observed interactions of the Four South nurses were different from those suggested by the literature in that most were not callous or detached. The themes emerging from the data suggest that these differences in observed behaviors may be due to the highly developed quality of caring observed. Nursing, as a culture, has shared values. Hospice, as a subculture of nursing, shares the value of caring. In fact, Stoddard (1978) describes hospice as a caring community.

At the close of the data collection period, I asked several of the nurses individually to define caring. Although caring was an essential component of the observed interactions, it was difficult for the nurses to define caring. As a tacit dimension of nursing, caring is experiential in nature and cannot be easily described in words.

It's subjective. You can't be objective and care or you don't have a heart.

Tender, loving care—physical, mental, religious.

Caring is the same for all the patients, whether or not they're hospice. The only difference is, maybe, the religious part. That's probably more important for the hospice [patients].

Caring is a true concern; as in "like" or "love"; a love for humanism and life.

Commitment to their humanness; totally separate from what's wrong with 'em.

You have to allow yourself to fall in love with each and every one of 'em.

These responses imply that caring is multidimensional and involves emotional commitment.

There are four possible explanations for the caring observed in the Four South nurses' interactions with their patients. The first is related to the fact that hospice nursing in general, and nursing on Four South in particular, does not emphasize the technological aspect of care. The lack of emphasis on high technology nursing leaves time available for caring. The second explanation is the fact that the Four South nurses verbalized a hospice identity. The focus of hospice is on care, rather than cure or high technology. The third explanation may be the nature of the individuals who have chosen to do this type of nursing. Perhaps people who choose to care for the dying have an innately caring nature. The last explanation is based on the observation that the Four South nurses each gave thought to the issues of life and death and consciously applied personal philosophies to their nursing interactions. Their nursing interactions were, therefore, filled with personal meaning and sharing and were enacted in a caring way.

It is probable that all four explanations were jointly responsible for the caring observed in the interactions between the Four South nurses and their patients.

Symbolic Interactionism and Caring

Nurses respond to speech and gestures based on the perceived meaning of these symbols. If nurses perceive all patients as human beings with similar basic needs, if they care about their patients as human beings, their responses will not vary based upon artificial boundaries. This means that if a nurse perceives all patients as sharing similar basic needs, the nurse will respond similarly to the symbolic acts of acutely and terminally ill patients. The commonality of care is founded on similar human needs.

The Effect of Busyness on Caring Behaviors

A complete absence of caring was never observed in any interaction. However, the extent of caring within interactions varied with the degree of "busyness," or amount of work required, of the nurses at any time; the busier the nurse, the less time available for caring behaviors. The following examples of one nurse's interactions with a terminally ill patient illustrate this point. The first of these interactions was observed on a day when there was an excessive amount of work for this nurse and the second on a day which was not quite so busy.

On an exceptionally busy day, Katie was to care for Mr. Brent, 62, a patient with brain cancer who was having difficulty accepting his terminal diagnosis. She heard the morning report on her patients and was making rounds, looking in on each before starting her morning care. When she reached the doorway of Mr. Brent's room he was in bed and Mrs. Brent was sitting at his bedside. Remaining in the doorway, Katie introduced herself.

Katie, RN: Good morning, Mr. Brent. My name is Katie and I'm your nurse today. How are you feeling?

Mr. Brent: Fine. [He looks at Katie as if she has no possible reason to ask such a question.] Do you think Father James will be around today? Oh! It's Friday and he's not here on Friday.

Mrs. Brent: [Pointing to Mr. Brent] He's been here so often that he knows everyone's schedule.

Katie, RN: Yes, I do remember you.

Mr. Brent: [To Mrs. Brent] Now, honey. Who is that priest that comes today? Is it the woman one [referring to the hospice chaplain]?

There was more talk about the chaplain.

Mr. Brent: I've always gone to church regularly. While I'm not religious, I try. [Mr. Brent looks intently at the Katie, waiting for a response.]

Katie, RN: [Changing the subject] How's your pain, Mr. Brent?

Mr. Brent: No pain. I'm great.

Katie, RN: I guess the pain medication is working. And that's why you're here.

Mr. Brent: I'm perfect. They can't find any cancer anywhere and that's why I feel good.

Mrs. Brent: [To Mr. Brent] Now, watch what you say. [Then, to Katie] He said that to the home nurse and she wrote down that he's confused and doesn't know he's sick. Now he does get confused from time to time. [She looks lovingly at Mr. Brent.] But he does know what's happening. What he means is that they can't find the primary site anywhere.

Mr. Brent: Even with all the scans.

Mrs. Brent: [To Mr. Brent] So the only place they've found the cancer is in your head.

Mr. Brent: And they can't cure it.

Katie, RN: But they can control it.

Mr. Brent: Yes. You know, we have no children. That's why we get along so well.

Katie, RN: Did you eat your breakfast?

Mr. Brent: I didn't like it.

Katie, RN: If you don't like what's on the menu you can order something else. For instance, you can always ask for fruit.

Katie continued to discuss the menu selection. Her interaction with Mr. and Mrs. Brent evaded the issues of the terminal aspect of Mr. Brent's illness and his covert references to his spiritual needs. Although both Mr. and Mrs. Brent alluded to these issues, Katie's focus of interaction on this busy morning was Mr. Brent's pain control and diet. Mr. Brent's cues for psychospiritual interaction were undeveloped.

The following day, however, when Four South was not as busy, Katie's interactions with Mr. Brent were quite different. Katie and he were discussing Mr. Brent's communication with his wife and the fact that he was concerned about Mrs. Brent's future well-being. After reminding him of the importance of discussing his feelings with his wife and telling his wife he loved her, Katie gently slipped her hand from Mr. Brent's, rose from the chair, and left the room. When out of Mr. Brent' sight, she wiped a tear from her eye and continued down the hallway (see page 33). Katie's behavior in this example reflected caring and concern about the Brents.

Busyness, as a dynamic, had a direct impact on the way nurses interacted with their patients, whether acutely or terminally ill. As shown in Chapter 5, busyness was affected by patient census and characteristics, staffing patterns, and familiarity with assigned patients. An increased amount of work required by the nurses affected the focus of care. The busier a nurse was, the less time she spent on caring interactions.

CONCLUSION

This research has demonstrated that it is possible for nurses to deal with a dichotomous patient population, providing comparable nursing care to groups of patients with seemingly disparate needs. Although the special needs of acutely ill and terminally ill patients may require different types of nursing, the basic need for caring remains the same for both types of patients. The interactive behaviors of the Four South nurses differed from the patterns described by Benoliel (1974) and Pillette (1980). This is not to say that the nurses previously described in those studies did not care about their patients. However, the nurses of Four South may have been better prepared, cognitively and affectively, for the special kind of nursing in which they engaged. In addition, they shared common personal values and philosophies of nursing and were usually given sufficient time to enact caring strategies and reflect upon these caring behaviors (Samarel, 1989a, 1989b). This combination of caring, preparedness, common ideology, and time made this group different.

LITERATURE CITED

American Nurses' Association. (1976). *Code for nurses with interpretive statements.* Kansas City, MO: Author.

Arndt, C., & Laeger, E. (1970). Role strain in a diversified role set. *Nursing Research, 19,* 253.

Benoliel, J. Q. (1974). Anticipatory grief in physicians and nurses. In B. Shoenberg (Ed.), *Anticipatory grief.* New York: Columbia University Press.

Brodish, M. S. (1982). Nursing practice conceptualized: An interaction model. *Image, 14*(1), 5–7.

Burger, S. (1980). Three approaches to patient care: Hospice, nursing homes, and hospitals. In M. Hamilton & H. Reid (Eds.), *A hospice handbook: A new way to care for the dying,* p. 132. Grand Rapids, MI: Eerdmans.

Caplan, R. D., & Jones, K. W. (1975). Effects of workload, role ambiguity, and type A personality on anxiety, depression, and heart rate. *Journal of Applied Psychology, 60,* 713.

Conway, M. E. (1978). Theoretical approaches to the study of roles. In M. E. Hardy & M. E. Conway (Eds.), *Role theory: Perspectives for health care professionals,* pp. 17–28. New York: Appleton-Century-Crofts.

Corwin, R. (1961). The professional employee: A study of conflict in nursing roles. *American Journal of Sociology, 66,* 604.

Glaser, B. G., & Strauss, A. L. (1979). *Awareness of dying.* New York: Aldine.

Hardy, M. E. (1978). Role stress and role strain. In M. E. Hardy & M. E. Conway (Eds.), *Role theory: Perspectives for health care professionals,* pp. 73–110. New York: Appleton-Century-Crofts.

Kramer, M. (1968). Role models, role conceptions, and role deprivation. *Nursing Research, 17,* 115.

Leininger, M. M. (1981). *Caring: An essential human need.* Thorofare, NJ: Charles B. Slack.

Lennard, H., & Bernstein, A. (1966). Expectations and behavior in therapy. In B. Biddle & E. Thomas (Eds.), *Role theory: Concepts and research.* New York: Wiley.

May, C. (1990). Research on nurse-patient relationships: Problems of theory, problems of practice. *Journal of Advanced Nursing, 15*(3), 307–315.

Meleis, A. I. (1975). Role insufficiency and role supplementation. *Nursing Research, 24,* 264–271.

Miles, R. H. (1975). An empirical test of causal interference between role perceptions of conflict and ambiguity and various personal outcomes. *Journal of Applied Technology, 60,* 334.

Overall, B., & Aronson, H. (1966). Expectations of psychotherapy in patients of lower socioeconomic class. In B. Biddle & E. Thomas (Eds.), *Role theory: Concepts and research.* New York: Wiley.

Pattison, E. M. (1978). The living-dying process. In C. A. Garfield (Ed.), *Psychological care of the dying patient.* New York: McGraw-Hill.

Peplau, H. E. (1952). *Interpersonal relations in nursing.* New York: Putnam.

Pillette, P. C. (1980). Caution: Objectivity and specialization may be hazardous to your humanity. *American Journal of Nursing, 9,* 1588–1590.

Samarel, N. (1989a). Caring for the living and dying: A study of role transition. *International Journal of Nursing Studies, 26,* 313–326.

Samarel, N. (1989b). Nursing in a hospital-base hospice unit: A study in caring. *Image, The Journal of Nursing Scholarship, 21,* 132–136.

Scott, R. (1969). Professional employees in a bureaucratic structure: Social work. In A. Etzioni (Ed.), *The semi-professions and their organizations.* New York: Free Press.

Snoek, J. D. (1966). Role strain in diversified role sets. *American Journal of Sociology, 71,* 363–372.

Stoddard, S. (1978). *The hospice movement.* New York: Vintage Books.

Watson, J. (1979). *Nursing: The philosophy and science of caring.* Boston: Little, Brown.

Williams, C. A. (1982). Role considerations in care of the dying patient. *Image, 14*(1), 8–11.

Young, D., & Jacobs, A. M. (1983). *Hospice nursing: A model curriculum for continuing education.* Los Angeles: California State University.

Chapter 7

Conclusion

SUMMARY

This research was a descriptive analysis of the interactive behaviors of a group of registered nurses caring for a population of patients considered typical of a hospital-based discrete hospice unit. The population included both terminally ill patients and patients expected to regain their health. Questions guiding the research related to role transitions in hospice nurses and the relations among the nurses' interactional behaviors, values, and philosophies. Nurses' interactions with acutely ill and terminally ill patients were analyzed within two dimensions of care: the biological and the psychospiritual. Analysis of the data revealed no differences in the ways the participant nurses interacted with acutely ill and terminally ill patients.

Role Transition

The observed interactions of the Four South nurses differed from those suggested by the literature on nurses' interactions with dying patients. Although role transition was required of the nurses, no role conflict or role insufficiency was observed. It is possible, then, to avoid these problems when dealing with a varying patient population. Although the special needs of acutely ill and terminally ill patients may generate different types of nursing tasks for these two groups, their basic need for caring remains the same. It was this commonality of caring that made it possible for the nurses on Four South to make role transitions without role conflict.

Caring

Humanistic caring was found to be the unifying focus of care for acutely ill and terminally ill patients, and to form the core of the nurses' shared values and nursing philosophies. A complete absence of caring was never observed in any interaction. However, the extent of the caring within interactions varied with the degree of "busyness," or work load of the Four South nurses at any particular time; the busier the nurse, the less time was available for caring behaviors.

Patient Responsiveness and Orientation

Caring behaviors diminished in interactions with unresponsive patients and with disoriented or confused patients. In such interactions, caring behaviors were predominantly nonverbal and limited to gentle touch in the course of providing physical care. Priorities of care varied for each patient, depending on the patient's responsiveness and orientation, which the nurses believed to determine his or her needs. The nurses believed that unresponsive or disoriented patients had different needs for nursing interaction than responsive and oriented patients.

Although all of the nurses had given considerable thought to the issue of death and had described their own notions of a "good death," this was not apparent in some of their interactions with patients. They dealt with the dying process differently in responsive and unresponsive patients. That is, they believed that only their responsive patients needed the nurse's presence to effect a "good death." Unresponsive patients whose families were present, however, were tended to in the same manner as those who were responsive. The nurses believed that, although the unresponsive patients needed little verbal interaction and support, their families did. Nurses' notions of a "good death," then, did not appear to apply to those patients who were alone and unresponsive.

These findings have implications for the increasing numbers of patients surviving head injuries, cerebral vascular accidents, and other neurological insults. Many of these patients experience transient or permanent alterations in responsiveness and orientation. While nurses in all settings may care for unresponsive or disoriented patients, these findings may be especially significant for operating room, recovery room, intensive care, and neurological nurses. Further investigation is needed to explore the possible reasons why nurses display different kinds of caring behaviors for responsive and unresponsive patients. The understanding gained from such an exploration may dramatically affect nursing care for patients experiencing alterations in responsiveness and orientation.

Symbolic Interactionism

The findings are congruent with the symbolic interactionist framework, according to which humans continually construct their social responses by interpreting the meanings of the stimuli they receive in social interactions (Blumer, 1969). These interpretations are dependent on a personal philosophy and value system. If nurses perceive patients as human beings having similar basic needs, they will respond similarly to acutely ill and terminally ill patients, the commonality of care being founded on the patients' human needs rather than on their differing prognoses. On the other hand, if nurses believe that unresponsive patients have different needs than responsive patients, their care for these two groups may vary. The Four South nurses believed that alert and responsive patients required different caring interactions than disoriented or unresponsive patients.

Specialized Preparation and Time

This research has also shown that the problems of role conflict and role insufficiency may be avoided through specialized preparation of nurses in both the affective and cognitive domains and by providing nurses enough time to reflect upon and enact their professional caring behaviors. Specialized preparation for the hospice nurses' dual role must include both hospice and acute care components in continuing professional education programs. Adequate time for caring behaviors may be provided through staffing patterns that allow a sufficiently low patient-nurse ratio and consistent staff assignments to enable nurses to be familiar with their assigned patients (see Chapter 6, Figure 2).

DISCUSSION

These findings are important not only for hospice nurses, but for all nurses caring for varying patient populations. Not unlike hospice nurses, medical-surgical nurses caring for both the acutely and terminally ill make role transitions, as do obstetrical nurses caring for mothers of healthy newborns and mothers of aborted fetuses, and mental health nurses caring for chronically impaired patients and patients experiencing acute psychiatric episodes. If these nurses do not care about their patients, have little continuing professional education geared to assisting them in meeting the needs of diverse patient populations, or have inadequate time to enact and reflect upon their professional behaviors, they may experience role conflict or role insufficiency. This would preclude smooth role transitions for these nurses, possibly leading to lack of motivation, poor quality of professional care, absenteeism, burnout, and attrition.

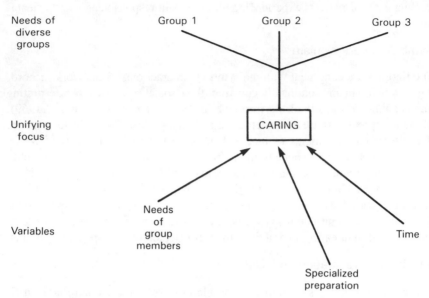

Figure 3 A model for role transition.

These findings imply that role conflict and insufficiency may be avoided through specialized professional preparation, provision of adequate time to perform and reflect upon professional duties, and a genuine caring about the needs of those served.

The model suggested in Figure 3 may be applicable to a variety of service professionals, both in health care and education. Caution must be exercised, however, in the generalization of these findings. The data generated by this research were based on observations of day nurses in a hospital-based discrete hospice unit in a suburban area of the Northeast. To generalize the findings to nurses outside such hospice settings, additional studies are needed. Replication is suggested in other hospice models, such as the scatter-bed hospice, in various geographic areas, and on all shifts. Generalization to nonhospice nurses and to other health-care providers requires replication in a variety of health care settings with observations of the entire health-care team.

LITERATURE CITED

Blumer, H. (1969). *Symbolic interactionism.* Englewood Cliffs: NJ: Prentice-Hall.

Method

THE DESIGN

I used an ethnographic method in this study. Ethnography, the systematic study of cultures, concentrates on repetitive patterns of behavior in natural settings where meaningful behavior occurs in context-dependent patterns. These patterns are understood from the subjects' point of view, discovered through long-term involvement by the researcher. This approach results in a deep understanding of a limited setting. Germain (1986), Leininger (1985), and Wilson (1989) provide helpful discussions of ethnographic method.

The purpose of an ethnographic study is to discover the cultural meaning of identified patterns of behavior. Nursing can be considered a culture, taught and learned in schools of nursing and reinforced in the institutional setting. A shared culture implies shared values, beliefs, behavior patterns, and expectations. Nursing ethnography attempts to discover the meanings that patterns of nursing behavior have to nurses. Unlike quantitative studies, which do not explore the unique perceptions of the subjects, ethnographic research can facilitate the subjective understanding of human behavior.

THE SETTING

Observations were made on a 35-bed unit in a 500-bed community hospital in a suburban area of the northeast United States. The unit of study had 10 beds in one area designated as hospice; the remaining 25 beds were considered general medical-surgical. In reality, however, hospice patients were placed throughout the unit for various reasons. These reasons included patient or family request for a private room (unavailable in the hospice area), need to be near the nurses' station, and unavailability of a bed in the hospice area. The registered nurses staffing this unit considered themselves hospice nurses. They adhered to a rotation of duty that placed each in the hospice area of the unit for four-week intervals. The remainder of the sixteen-week rotation was within the medical-surgical area of the unit.

Ten nurses were invited to participate in the study and all ten agreed. All patients admitted to the unit, both terminal and acute, were requested to participate in the research. Patients were observed as part of the dyad of interaction with nurses. The focus of the study, however, was on the nurses in the nurse-patient interaction.

PROTECTION OF HUMAN SUBJECTS

Each attending physician admitting patients to Four South at Madison Medical Center was informed by mail of the nature of the study. Each was asked to grant me written consent to invite his or her patients to participate in the research.

Explanations of the research were given to all the nurses participating in the study. Patients, too, received an explanation of the research upon admission to the unit. In instances where patients were incompetent, that is, admitted by a family member who authorized treatment, the family member signing consent received the explanation of the research. A copy of the explanation, in writing, was retained by each nurse, patient, or family member. Explanations included the major purpose of the study, method of data collection, assurance of confidentiality, and permission to withdraw at any time. The informed consent was signed only after the explanation had been discussed with me and questions had been answered to the complete satisfaction of the participants.

TECHNIQUES OF DATA COLLECTION

The primary mode of data collection in ethnographic method is participant observation. Pearsall (1965) describes the role continuum for participant observers, a continuum ranging from complete observer to complete participant. In the observer-as-participant role the researcher remains detached and objective; observation takes precedence. In the participant-as-observer role, close interpersonal relationships may be developed with the informants. While a degree of objectivity may be lost, the observer enters the social and cultural milieu of the informants and enjoys a wider range of information.

During the orienting phase of fieldwork I was present on the unit one day weekly. The day varied from week to week to give me an idea of staffing patterns on various days, but it was always scheduled in advance with the unit's clinical coordinator or assistant clinical coordinator. Observations were usually made over three-hour periods at varying times to provide opportunity to observe the staff and the unit throughout the entire day.

These initial months of observation were spent in the hallways, nurses' station, nurses' lounge, and offices. I attempted to be as unobtrusive as possible—a "complete observer"—during this orienting phase so as to allow the staff to become accustomed to and accept my presence.

My role in this study ranged from observer-as-participant to participant-as-observer. During this early phase of data collection a lab coat with a name pin identifying me as a registered nurse was worn over street clothes. The type of data gathered included information on the physical structure of the unit, routine of the unit, staffing and census patterns, hospice policy and procedure, and acute care policy. Observations were also made at unit staff and team meetings.

Within a few months my presence was beginning to be accepted by staff as natural. Observations of interactions between nurses, physicians, and other team members were recorded on a memo pad out of sight of the informants. I then began to take a more active role (observer-as-participant), as I came to be included in conversations among staff and participated, to some degree, in informal patient care conferences in which patients' needs were discussed and nursing care was planned. My participation in these conferences was minimal, being limited to questions about patients' conditions and care.

Observations of actual nurse-patient interactions began in the sixth month of the study. I was present on the unit two or three days weekly for the next five months. My role evolved to that of a participant-as-observer at this point, as I provided the nurses assistance with aspects of patient care such as moving, bathing, or bed making. I was a participant-as-observer only in the presence of another nurse; I assumed no patient responsibility whatsoever.

Because active participation contributes to greater understanding of observed behaviors (Bogdan & Taylor, 1975; Leininger, 1985; Pearsall, 1965; Spradley, 1980), I dressed in a manner similar to the nursing staff. For hygienic reasons, a uniform was appropriate for direct patient care. The uniform also made me less obtrusive to both patients and staff.

When I was not actively participating in patient care, I "shadowed" a participant nurse as she cared for and interacted with patients. In addition, I continued my observations in the lounge, hallways, offices, and nurses' station.

Notes recorded on a small memo pad were kept to a minimum and not recorded in the presence of the participants. Detailed field notes were written immediately after leaving the unit.

During the period of data collection, I observed over 282 nurse-patient interactions with both acutely ill and terminally ill patients. Of these observations, 135 involved acutely ill patients and 147 involved those who were terminally ill. Of the 147 terminally ill patients, 108 had a diagnosis of cancer in some form. I also observed nurse-nurse and nurse-physician interactions regarding their patients.

Other methods of data collection used were informal interviews and demographic questionnaires. Informal interviews, both structured and semistructured, were used with all nurses during the period of investigation. The foci of the structured interviews were personal values, philosophies of nursing, and perceptions of patient needs. Semistructured interviews were utilized for participant validation of observed phenomena. The semistructured interviews often took the form of impromptu discussions in various locations throughout the unit. Semistructured interviews were also conducted with social workers, physicians, nurse's aides, the unit secretary, and the director of the hospice team. The interviews varied and were planned at some times, serendipitous at others.

Each participant nurse was requested, on a voluntary basis, to complete a demographic questionnaire, that included information such as age, type of basic nursing education, years of nursing experience, duration of hospice experience, and religious affiliation. It was explained to each nurse that these variables can affect the way nurses interact with patients. All participant nurses completed the questionnaires.

In addition to participant observation, interviews, and demographic questionnaires, supporting documents such as nurses' notes, job descriptions, and staff development programs were reviewed.

Strategies for maximizing validity and reliability were carefully planned. Repetition of observation and prolonged involvement, along with periods of intermittent observation that minimized note taking in the presence of the participants, reduced the observer effect. The principle of observational inclusiveness was observed by focusing on all the nurses on the day shift of the unit. To reduce the effect of my perceptual biases, data were reconstructed by informants and observed phenomena were confirmed in informal semistructured interviews with participant nurses. In these interviews nurses were asked for their perceptions of events as shortly after their occurrence as possible. Verbatim quotes that provided concrete and precise descriptions of events facilitated the description of phenomena.

These strategies ensured an authentic representation of the professional interactive patterns of the hospice nurses observed.

DATA ANALYSIS

The field notes were analyzed systematically using Glaser's (1978) constant comparative method of qualitative analysis. Nurses' interactions with acutely ill and terminally ill patients were compared in a search for patterns. As data from participant observations and interviews were being collected, coded, and analyzed, emerging patterns of interaction suggested themes regarding nurses' interactions with their patients. As patterns and themes began to emerge from the data, theoretical sampling allowed me to elaborate the developing codes and to predict the nature of the observed interactions. For example, as differences in nurses' observed interactional patterns with responsive and unresponsive patients began to emerge from the data, I purposely arranged to observe each nurse as she interacted with both types of patients. In this way, sufficient data were obtained to confirm, validate, and expand emergent patterns and themes. It became possible to predict how nurses would interact with responsive and unresponsive patients.

LITERATURE CITED

Bogdan, R., & Taylor, S. J. (1975). *Introduction to qualitative research methods.* New York: John Wiley.

Germain, C. (1986). Ethnography: The method. In P. L. Munhall & C. J. Oiler (Eds.), *Nursing research: A qualitative perspective,* pp. 147–162. Norwalk, CT: Appleton-Century-Crofts.

Glaser, B. G. (1978). *Theoretical sensitivity.* Mill Valley, CA: Sociology Press.

Leininger, M. M. (1985). *Qualitative research methods in nursing.* Orlando, FL: Grune & Stratton.

Pearsall, M. (1965). Participant observation as role and method in behavioral research. *Nursing Research,* 14, 37–42.

Spradley, J. P. (1980). *Participant observation.* New York: Holt, Rinehart, and Winston.

Wilson, H. S. (1989). *Research in nursing.* Redwood City, CA: Addison-Wesley.

The Fieldwork

MY BACKGROUND

People have continually asked me why I would choose to study care for the dying. Most view death as a depressing subject. Why would anyone choose to study dying or nursing the dying? Thinking about what led me in this direction caused me to examine my nursing background.

My clinical nursing background is a unique combination of critical care and hospice care. As a critical care nurse for several years, part of my job entailed taking my turn as a member of the "code team" in my hospital. When it was my turn to "cover codes," I attended all respiratory or cardiac arrests occurring on my shift. I shared responsibility for performing cardiopulmonary resuscitation, starting intravenous lines, administering emergency medications, defibrillation, and other procedures designed to save patients' lives. Working in critical care and covering codes was satisfying and challenging. When a patient died in spite of our efforts, however, it was often viewed as a personal failure; the nurses, doctors, and health care system had failed that patient.

I soon began to wonder what the other side of the spectrum was all about. I knew what saving lives was about. What would it be like to help people die? Death is the natural end to all life and yet it seemed to be denied by all those with whom I worked, including myself. This question, more of a rumination, continued to nag at my thoughts and eventually led me to work as a community-health hospice nurse, visiting terminally ill patients in their homes and helping their families to care for them. This explains my clinical focus on hospice care in my initial graduate work. I saw a different kind of nursing here and began to ask questions about nurses who care for dying patients. I wanted to understand their thoughts, feelings, motives, and outlooks.

Early in my doctoral study, I decided that I needed to learn more about qualitative research. It seemed to me that the only way to learn about the human situation, was to obtain the perspective of the very people I wanted to understand. I believed that it was only from their perspective, not from mine, that their feelings, motives, and intentions could be understood. I also believed, and still do, that nursing research is in its infancy. If our research objective is to improve nursing care, we must first obtain a thorough understanding of the objects and subjects of that care, i.e., nurses and patients. These beliefs, along with my own unusual critical care and hospice background, led me to ask the questions examined in the present work.

GAINING ENTRANCE

Once I was reasonably certain what it was that I wanted to study, I explored various agencies as possible data collection sites. I decided to return to Madison Medical Center (MMC), the hospital where I had worked as a critical care nurse. MMC's hospice seemed ideal in that it met all the hospice criteria of the National Hospice Organization and had a sufficient patient census and hospice staff to provide the necessary data.

I met with the hospital nursing administration and with the hospice administration. They were not only receptive to the idea of supporting my research but were also quite enthusiastic and offered their support. Before I could proceed any further, however, I needed to have the approval of my university's human subjects review board, the MMC human subjects review board, and the MMC Nursing Research Committee. There were no problems obtaining approval from all three. Although this was encouraging, I felt that my biggest challenge would be the hospice nurses. The data collection would require my presence on the hospice unit two or three days each week for one to two years. I would be ever-present and, perhaps, ever in the way. Why would a group of nurses consent to such a nuisance? Would they see the data collection as an invasion of their privacy?

My fears were unfounded. The entire staff on Four South—nurses, aides, and secretaries—welcomed the opportunity to participate in the study. They saw my research as having the potential to improve patient care. At this point, I thought I was home free. Wrong!

MMC's research policy gave attending physicians the right to decide whether their private patients could be invited to participate in any research project at the hospital. This meant that I needed to contact each attending physician, explain the study and the research procedures, and request permission to invite that physician's patients to participate in the study. Actually, the only participation required of patients was to allow me to observe their nurses provide care. Several physicians returned the signed consent to me without any further questions. The majority, however, were quite protective toward their patients and had many questions for me. Most were satisfied that the research posed no risk for their patients and agreed to allow their patients to participate. Four physicians believed my observations would be an unnecessary invasion of their patients' privacy and refused to allow their patients to participate in the research.

Once approval had been obtained from the hospital administration, the nursing administration, the human subjects review board, the nurses, and the physicians, I needed to approach the patients on Four South. Upon my arrival on the unit each morning, I obtained a census sheet listing all the patients, their ages, room numbers, and physicians' names. Those patients of the four physicians not consenting to the research were omitted from the list and no observations of nurses were made in their rooms. I approached all other patients, provided an explanation of the research, answered their questions, and obtained signed consent. When patients refused consent, which occurred very infrequently, they were assured that their refusal was understood. Because those patients refusing consent were usually quite apologetic and seemed to feel bad about "thwarting" my research, I attempted to visit each on a future day just to say hello. This seemed to convince them that their refusal was truly accepted.

In instances where patients were incompetent to give consent, the family member authorizing medical treatment was approached with an explanation of the research and requested to consent. If no family member was available, no observations were made in the patient's room.

A record was kept of all patients approached, all who consented, and all who refused. This record was used on subsequent observation days. Each time a patient was readmitted to Four South after being discharged, he or she was again provided with an explanation of the research and invited to participate. Of the seven patients who refused to participate, four were readmitted during the period of the research. I did not approach them on their readmissions, as I did not want them to feel coerced or pressured in any way. However, one of these patients approached me on a subsequent admission and requested to participate in the research. He received a complete explanation and provided signed consent.

Obtaining initial approval to collect data, providing explanations to each patient, obtaining their signed consent, and maintaining complete records were more time consuming than I had ever imagined.

GETTING STARTED

During the initial, or orienting phase of the fieldwork, my primary objective was to become an accepted part of Four South.

Early in the fieldwork, the nurses viewed me as a celebrity. They were impressed that I was a doctoral student and flattered that I had chosen their unit for my research. Whenever I arrived nurses would approach me, ask how the research was going, and offer me coffee and their hospitality. This was problematic for two reasons. First, in order to eliminate observer effects, it was necessary that the staff cease to notice me. Second, I feared that I was disrupting the unit routine and the clinical coordinator might raise objections to my presence. I attempted to handle this situation with tact and patience. Realizing that it would take time to go unnoticed, I waited. With regard to the hospitality, I would thank the staff and explain that I needed to get started on my research. I would busy myself reviewing procedure manuals or doing "paperwork" in the area of the nurses' station. I hoped it would appear to the staff that I was busy and not attending to my surroundings; in fact, I was observing the unit routine.

After some time passed, it appeared that my presence on Four South was accepted as normal. The following incident, however, made me realize that I still needed to wait and to be patient. I was quietly observing the unit routine at the nurses' station when there was a phone call for one of the nurses. The secretary asked if I would mind letting the nurse know about the call and directed me to an unoccupied room down the hall where the nurse was making a bed. As I approached the room, I overheard two nurses in conversation. When they saw me, the conversation changed dramatically from a discussion about the weather to a discussion about the progress of my research. I learned that my presence was still unusual to the staff and that I needed to give it more time.

Over a period of several months, the nurses' attitudes toward my presence on the unit steadily changed. From viewing me as a celebrity and making a fuss over me, they came to view me as a frequent guest and finally as nothing out of the ordinary. The following exchange between one of the nurses and a patient exemplifies the latter:

Patient: [To his nurse] Who is that?

Nurse: Oh, that's just Nelda.

At last, I realized I was making progress.

Another problem I encountered was setting boundaries for my participation. As discussed in Appendix A, my role ranged from observer-as-participant to participant-as-observer. I explained to the Four South nurses that I would be *assisting them* at the bedside from time to time in the process of my observations. On several occasions, however, nurses would request me to move or to bathe a patient with no assistance from them. My purpose on the unit was to observe nurse-patient interactions, not to provide nursing care, and I needed to set limits on my participation in order to meet my research goals. I did not want to refuse assistance to the nurses making those requests for fear of alienating them from me. My response, in these situations, was always accepted without question: "I would love to help you in any way I am able. However, because I am not on staff here, I am limited in what I am permitted to do. I am permitted to assist with patient care only in the presence of a licensed staff nurse." The nurse usually responded with an apology and an explanation that she knew that but had forgotten it. I realized that, had I not set limits on my participation, I might have spent the entire period of data collection providing patient care rather than making observations.

DOING THE FIELDWORK

Reflecting back on the research process, particularly the data collection and analysis, I have learned much, not only about hospice nurses' interactive behaviors, but also about the process of doing fieldwork.

I also learned that the guidance of more experienced researchers is needed to initiate data collection. The major purposes of the initial phase of data collection are to familiarize the investigator with the research setting, to feel comfortable with the participants, and to have the researcher's presence accepted by the participants. Familiarization with the research setting had been practiced in preparatory courses in ethnographic methodology and was a skill easily transferred. A feeling of comfort with the nurses and their acceptance of my presence, however, were more difficult and time consuming to attain. Acceptance and comfort were attained not by specific techniques but by spending much time with the participants and by waiting, very patiently, for them to stop noticing me. This waiting period was occasionally awkward for me, as it seemed that nothing tangible was being accomplished. That is, I feared that if it were perceived that I wasn't "doing anything" it would become difficult to justify my continual presence on the hospice unit.

During this awkward stage, guidance from researchers who had recently been through this same process and had experienced similar feelings of inadequacy was invaluable. For this reason I strongly suggest that researchers inexperienced in fieldwork have someone on whom they can rely for support, especially in the initial phases of data collection.

In addition to learning about the fieldwork process, I gained insight into the manner in which phenomena and, in fact, life are perceived. The emphasis on viewing phenomena from the perspective of one's research subjects reinforced my conviction that events may not always be as they appear. Alternative perspectives, particularly those of other individuals, always need to be considered prior to making firm judgments about the world in which we live.

If asked for advice from someone beginning doctoral research, I would observe that fieldwork is time consuming—much more so than other types of research—and tedious, particularly the writing of the meticulous field notes needed for valid data analysis. The process can also be immensely enjoyable. Qualitative studies such as this one have the potential of contributing to the investigator's personal growth by imparting a deep understanding of the lives, or part of the lives, of others. This is well worth the required investment of time and patience.

Review of the Literature Relevant to the Study

I reviewed the hospice literature in preparation for this study. This review included both the history of hospice and an exploration of current hospice trends. To understand fully how the concept of caring has served as the unifying focus for the nursing care of terminally ill and acutely ill patients, I examined the caring literature as well.

HOSPICE

Origins of Hospice Care

Hospice had its origin before the Christian era. The concept of caring for travelers and the needy in a hospice dates back more than 2000 years to Syria and Rome (Stoddard, 1978). A hospice was a way station where weary pilgrims, or travelers, stopped for several days to rest and be nourished. In fact, the word hospice is derived from the Latin *hospes,* meaning both a guest and a host (Buckingham, 1983). Stoddard (1978) has drawn an interesting analogy between the pilgrim needing assistance on the journey and the dying person needing assistance toward death. The dying person is viewed as a traveler moving forward; death is viewed as a transformation.

Despite its origins in antiquity, the hospice is not a long-standing concept in the United States. The needs of the sick and dying in the United States in recent years have been met in institutional settings; Davidson (1979) estimates that 90% of those dying in the early 1970s spent their last days or months either in a nursing home or in an acute care facility. Acute care facilities are not designed to support the process of dying. They are intended, instead, to provide aggressive treatment to save lives. It is just as destructive, however, to overtreat the incurable as to neglect to treat the curable; life-saving techniques are inappropriate for the terminally ill (Stoddard, 1978).

The consequences of institutionalization of the terminally ill are several. Estrangement from family leads to feelings of abandonment (Davidson, 1979). To be alone at the time of death is undesirable, for the dying process is difficult and requires the assistance of significant others (Kubler-Ross, 1970). Hospitals and nursing homes, in addition, have not succeeded in managing uncontrolled or intractable pain. This has resulted in much suffering and dehumanization of the terminally ill.

Institutionalization of these patients has a negative effect on families as well. Separation from the dying and from the concept of death has resulted in much misunderstanding of the mourning process (Kubler-Ross, 1970). There is a need to assist the living to deal with death in order to avoid separation from the dying process and the resultant misunderstanding that accompanies this separation.

Not until the past several years has our awareness of death and dying grown through courses, films, books, and studies (primarily the work of Dr. Elisabeth Kubler-Ross). This new awareness has been reflected by the growth of the hospice, providing health care and support services to terminally ill patients and their families. In 1975 the majority of hospices in the United States were home care teams where services were provided for the entire family and extended to the period of bereavement (Wald, Foster, & Wald, 1980). In 1978 the birth of the National Hospice Organization (NHO) was a major step in the hospice health care system. The NHO was begun in response to the needs of new hospice programs; its task is to oversee the development of hospice care in the United States and Canada. The NHO's functions are to describe the hospice concept and function; to establish licensure, accreditation and review guidelines for hospice care; and to develop reimbursement criteria for hospice programs (NHO, 1978, pp. 1–2).

A Model Hospice

St. Christopher's Hospice in London, established in 1962, is the universal model of the modern-day hospice (Stoddard, 1978). The creed of St. Christopher's hospice is to allow dying patients to remain without pain, alert, and in control of themselves. This is achieved through the self-administration, for as long as possible, of a special "hospice mix," a combination of medications designed not to relieve but to prevent pain without causing loss of consciousness. Another necessary ingredient to the hospice experience is the integration of life, meaning the natural combination of various aspects of living through the maintenance of an intergenerational environment including children, pets, enjoyed possessions, and a home-like atmosphere.

Religion and faith (not necessarily in God) also play an important role at St. Christopher's Hospice. The individual is viewed as a three-dimensional being: biological, psychological, and spiritual. Hospice care focuses on the psychological and spiritual dimensions of the individual, while permitting the biological process to follow its natural course.

Though no statistics are available to document the exact number of home care and inpatient hospices currently in operation, NHO's executive director informed me that the number of inpatient and home care hospice programs is growing steadily in response to our awakening awareness of the necessary function they serve. Many of the new hospices are modeled on St. Christopher's.

CARING

Caring Defined

Caring is an interactive process that helps another person grow toward self-actualization (Leininger, 1980; Mayeroff, 1971). In true caring, devotion must be present; devotion is manifested by lending one's total attention to the object of devotion and by accepting obligations. Ingredients of caring include knowledge, alternating rhythms of activity and inactivity, patience, honesty, trust, humility, hope, courage, and selflessness.

According to Leininger (1980, p. 136), caring includes "those human acts and processes which provide assistance to another individual or group based on an interest in or concern for that human being, or to meet an expressed, obvious, or anticipated need."

Caring may be scientific—that is, based upon knowledge—or humanistic and based upon "philosophic, phenomenologic, and objective and subjective experiential feelings and acts of assisting others" (Leininger, 1980, p. 136). These acts reflect inherent qualities of the caregiver identified as empathetic, protective, supportive, compassionate, succorant, and educational. Caring denotes concern, devotion, and commitment and is expressed nonverbally more so than verbally (Leininger, 1980, 1981).

Certain basic premises or assumptions about caring have been identified by Leininger (1984) and Watson (1979):

- Although caring is a universal phenomenon, the expressions of caring are transmitted culturally and vary among different cultures.
- Caring acts and processes are essential for human birth, development, growth, survival, and peaceful death and result in satisfaction of human needs.
- Caring is interpersonal.
- Care is multidimensional; it includes biological, sociocultural, psychological, spiritual, and environmental dimensions.

Watson (1979) has identified ten carative factors: (a) a humanistic value system based on kindness, concern, and love; (b) the ability to instill faith and hope in another; (c) sensitivity to self and others, allowing oneself to recognize and feel emotions; (d) the ability to establish a helping relationship; (e) acceptance of the expression of feelings, both positive and negative; (f) use of the scientific method of decision making, which may be condensed into the nursing process; (g) an interpersonal focus on teaching and learning to provide information and reduce stress; (h) the provision of a multidimensionally supportive environment; (i) facilitation of the gratification of human needs, and (j) allowance for existential or phenomenological forces, recognizing that some problems are insoluble and that such situations have personal meaning for the participants. In the last instance, the caregiver helps the one cared for to understand the situation and is concerned with the unique experiences of the individual. From an existential viewpoint, the caregiver uses the language of experience to explain the experience of the one cared for. Helping someone to face death, therefore, requires coming to terms with one's own death.

Caring has been described as an art (Bevis, 1981) and as an attitude (Noddings, 1984) and implies a commitment to serve the one cared for. According to Bevis (1981, p. 50), "Caring is a feeling . . . [that] motivates and energizes action." Feelings are converted into behaviors that help improve the state of being of the one cared for. Gaut (1981) maintains, however, that caring cannot be described as a behavior or a set of behaviors, but must be understood through the significance of acts expressing specific attitudes and meanings on the part of the actors. Finally, caring has been described as a reverence for life (Hyde, 1977).

Caring is an interactive process involving the opening of oneself to another. It requires risk taking and courage. The process of caring has two components: an activities aspect that involves assisting or performing duties; and an attitudinal aspect underlying the way the activities are performed. The two characteristics necessary to maintain a caring attitude are maturity and self-awareness (Blattner, 1981; Griffin, 1983; Parse, 1981).

The stimulus, or motivation, for caring may be any one or a combination of three: moral (conforming to a standard), innate (reflecting the essential nature of a person), or cognitive (based on knowledge or awareness) (Gustafson, 1984).

Caring in Nursing

Care, cure, and coordination are the essential components of nursing. The care component includes both caring for and caring about the patient (American Nurses' Association, 1965; Brunner & Suddarth, 1975).

As a science of caring, professional nursing practice requires a combination of scientific knowledge and a humanistic value system (Watson, 1979, 1981, 1988; Watson & Ray, 1988). Professional caring is defined by Leininger (1981, p. 9) as "those cognitive and culturally learned action behaviors, techniques, processes, or patterns that enable an individual, family, or community to improve or maintain a favorably healthy condition or lifeway." These enabling behaviors are expressed in interpersonal relationships between nurse and patient that extend beyond the physical care provided by the nurse. Thus the nurse-patient relationship is the essence of nursing care (Johnson, Dumas, & Johnson, 1967). Riemen (1983) has described three characteristics of a caring interaction in nursing: (a) the nurse is existentially present, that is, her attention is fully with the patient; (b) the nurse listens and responds in an unsolicited manner; and (c) the patient feels comfort and relaxation as a result. Gustafson (1984) and Gaut (1984) have also emphasized the importance of action and interaction as aspects of professional care.

Caring in Hospice

The deep caring required in hospice settings must embrace the spiritual dimension. To truly care for the dying, caretakers must face the reality of their own death, thus facilitating establishment of a bond between the dying patient and the nurse (Donovan, 1979). Caring for the terminally ill patient requires this special bond; caring for the acutely ill patient does not.

Caring for acutely ill patients is also differentiated from caring for terminally ill patients by the concepts of care and cure, as articulated by Benoliel (1972, p. 202):

> Whereas the concept of cure centers on the treatment of disease, the concept of care has at its core a concern about the welfare and well-being of the person. Cure deals with the objective aspects of the case. Somewhat in contrast, care deals with the subjective meanings of the disease experience. Cure has its origins in science and instrumentation; care has its roots in human compassion and respect for the special needs of persons in a vulnerable condition.

Unfortunately, technical advances in health care, combined with the problems of third party payment and constraints on health care expenditures, have resulted in a curing syndrome with less and less emphasis on the caring aspects of health care, particularly the special caring needs of terminally ill patients (as described by Benoliel, 1972, and Donovan, 1979). Hospice nursing, however, preserves the caring aspect of care. This is possible because nurses caring for the terminally ill are less preoccupied with high-technology nursing procedures and are, therefore, permitted to focus on the more human, carative aspects of nursing.

LITERATURE CITED

American Nurses' Association. (1965). *Educational preparation for nurse practitioners and assistants to nurses: A position paper.* New York: Author.

Benoliel, J. Q. (1972). The concept of care for a child with leukemia. *Nursing Forum,* 11(2), 194–204.

Bevis, E. O. (1981). Caring: A life force. In M. M. Leininger (Ed.), *Caring: An essential human need,* pp. 49–59. Thorofare, NJ: Charles B. Slack.

Blattner, B. (1981). *Holistic nursing.* Englewood Cliffs, NJ: Prentice-Hall.

Boyle, J. S. (1981). An application of the structural-functional method to the phenomenon of caring. In M. M. Leininger (Ed.), *Caring: An essential human need,* pp. 37–47. Thorofare, NJ: Charles B. Slack.

Brunner, L. S., & Suddarth, D. S. (1975). *Textbook of medical-surgical nursing.* Philadelphia: J. B. Lippincott.

Buckingham, R. W. (1983). *The complete hospice guide.* New York: Harper & Row.

Davidson, G. (1979). *Dying: Facing the facts.* New York: McGraw-Hill.

Donovan, H. (1979). Mind-heart work: Caring for the dying. *Supervisor Nurse,* 10(9), 20–23.

Gaut, D. A. (1981). Conceptual analysis of caring: Research method. In M. M. Leininger (Ed.), *Caring: An essential human need,* pp. 17–24. Thorofare, NJ: Charles B. Slack.

Gaut, D. A. (1984). A theoretic description of caring as action. In M. M. Leininger (Ed.), *Care: The essence of nursing and health,* pp. 27–44. Thorofare, NJ: Charles B. Slack.

Griffin, A. P. (1983). A philosophical analysis of caring in nursing. *Journal of Advanced Nursing,* 8(4), 289–295.

Gustafson, W. (1984). Motivational and historical aspects of care and nursing. In M. M. Leininger (Ed.), *Care: The essence of nursing and health,* pp. 61–73. Thorofare, NJ: Charles B. Slack.

Hyde, A. (1977). The phenomenon of caring (Part 6). *Nursing Research Report,* 12(2), 2.

Johnson, J., Dumas, R., & Johnson, B. (1967). Interpersonal relations: The essence of nursing care. *Nursing Forum,* 6(3), 324–334.

Kubler-Ross, E. (1970). *On death and dying.* New York: Macmillan.

Leininger, M. M. (1980). Caring: A central focus of nursing and health care services. *Nursing and Health Care,* 1(3), 135–143, 176.

Leininger, M. M. (1981). *Caring: An essential human need.* Thorofare, NJ: Charles B. Slack.

Leininger, M. M. (1984). *Care: The essence of nursing and health.* Thorofare, NJ: Charles B. Slack.

Mayeroff, M. (1971). *On caring.* New York: Harper & Row.

National Hospice Organization. (1978). *Hospice standards.* St. Paul, MN: Author.

Noddings, N. (1984). *Caring*. Berkeley: University of California Press.

Parse, R. R. (1981). Caring from a human science perspective. In M. M. Leininger (Ed.), *Caring: An essential human need*, pp. 129–132. Thorofare, NJ: Charles B. Slack.

Ray, M. A. (1981). A philosophical analysis of caring within nursing. In M. M. Leininger (Ed.), *Caring: An essential human need*, pp. 25–36. Thorofare, NJ: Charles B. Slack.

Riemen, D. J. (1983). The essential structure of a caring interaction: A phenomenological study (Doctoral dissertation, Texas Women's University). *Dissertation Abstracts International*, 44, 3041B.

Stoddard, S. (1978). *The hospice movement*. New York: Vintage Books.

Wald, F., Foster, Z., & Wald, H. (1980). The hospice movement as a health care reform. *Nursing Outlook*, 28, 173–178.

Watson, J. (1979). *Nursing: The philosophy and science of caring*. Boston: Little, Brown.

Watson, J. (1981). Some issues related to a science of caring for nursing practice. In M. M. Leininger (Ed.), *Caring: An essential human need*, pp. 61–67. Thorofare, NJ: Charles B. Slack.

Watson, J. (1988). *Nursing: Human science and human care*. New York: National League for Nursing.

Watson, J., & Ray, M. A. (Eds.). (1988). *The ethics of care and the ethics of cure: Synthesis in chronicity*. New York: National League for Nursing.

BIBLIOGRAPHY

Benner, P., & Wrubel, J. (1988). Caring comes first. *American Journal of Nursing*, 88(8), 1072–1075.

Constantino, R. E. (1989). Care and caring: The concepts explored. *Phillipine Nursing Journal*, 59(2), 11–23.

Didich, J., & Weick, J. K. (1989). The development of a palliative care program. *Cleveland Clinic Journal of Medicine*, 56(8), 762–764.

Dobratz, M. C. (1990). Hospice nursing: Present perspectives and future directives. *Cancer Nursing*, 13(2), 116–122.

Dush, D. M. (1988). Psychological research in hospice care: Toward specificity of therapeutic mechanisms. *Hospice Journal*, 4(2), 9–36.

Forrest, D. (1989). The experience of caring. *Journal of Advanced Nursing*, 14(10), 815–823.

Fry, S. T. (1988). The ethic of caring: Can it survive in nursing? *Nursing Outlook*, 36(1), 48.

Fry, S. T. (1989). Toward a theory of nursing ethics. *Advances in Nursing Science*, 11(4), 9–22.

Gabriel, R. M. (1988). Advancing the state of hospice care: A continuum of research methodologies. *Hospice Journal*, 4(3), 73–82.

Gallman, L. (1988). *Caring: A concept in nursing*. New York: National League for Nursing.

Hull, M. M. (1989). Family needs and supportive nursing behaviors during terminal cancer: A review. *Oncology Nursing Forum*, 16(6), 787–792.

Krysl, M., & Watson, J. (1988). Existential moments of caring: Facets of nursing and social support. *Advances in Nursing Science,* 10(2), 12–17.

McBride, A. B. (1989). Knowledge about care and caring: State of the art and future development. *Reflections,* 15(2), 5–7.

Moccia, P. (1988). At the faultline: Social activism and caring. *Nursing Outlook,* 36(1), 30–33.

Roberts, J. E. (1990). Uncovering hidden caring. *Nursing Outlook,* 38(2), 67–69.

Schraff, S. H. (1988). *The hospice concept.* New York: National League for Nursing.

Smerke, J. (1989). *Interdisciplinary guide to the literature for human caring.* New York: National League for Nursing.

Tanner, C. A. (1990). Caring as a value in nursing education. *Nursing Outlook,* 38(2), 70–72.

Warren, L. D. (1988). Review and synthesis of nine nursing studies on care and caring. *Journal of the New York State Nurses' Association,* 19(4), 10–16.

Watson, J. (1988). New dimensions of human caring theory. *Nursing Science Quarterly,* 1(4), 175–181.

Watson, J. (1990). The moral failure of the patriarchy. *Nursing Outlook,* 38(2), 62–66.

Index